THE BULLYING PREVENTION HANDBOOK:

A GUIDE FOR PRINCIPALS, TEACHERS, AND COUNSELORS

JOHN H. HOOVER
THE UNIVERSITY OF NORTH DAKOTA
CENTER FOR TEACHING AND LEARNING

RONALD OLIVER

NATIONAL EDUCATIONAL SERVICE
BLOOMINGTON, INDIANA   1996

Copyright © 1996 by National Educational Service
1252 Loesch Road
Bloomington, Indiana 47404
(812) 336-7700
(888) 763-9045 (toll free)
e-mail: nes@nesonline.com
www.nesonline.com

Cover design by Bill Dillon

Printed in the United States of America

Printed on recycled paper

ISBN 1-879639-44-0

DEDICATION

From John

I would like to dedicate this book to all children who have suffered at the hands of their peers and especially to the memory of Brian Head. I recognize with great appreciation the mentoring I received from Kristen Juul—a gentle soul who deeply cares about children. To my co-author and friend, Ron Oliver: I am more complete for having known you.

I thank my mother and father for instilling a sense of right and wrong, which has helped me see bullying for what it is. Most of all, I'd like to thank my family for their love and support: My wife Betsy and my children Amelia, Ray, and Don.

From Ron

To those who went before without a voice to complain or whine, to those who suffered bravely but silently, to those who knew better all along that might does not make right and that masculinity does not equal violence against any child anywhere, and finally to my writing partner, Dr. John H. Hoover, my complementary, complimentary fellow, I wish to dedicate this book.

TABLE OF CONTENTS

FOREWORD

The Bullying Prevention Handbook is a wonderful resource for addressing bully/victim problems during the pre-adolescent and adolescent years. Those of us who work in the field know the fear and pain many students silently endure. But until now no one had systematically collected data on this subject. The authors, John Hoover and Ronald Oliver, provide sound research to document that students in the United States report the middle school years as the worst years in terms of the intensity of bullying experienced. This handbook is far more, however, than a review of the problem; it is a comprehensive approach that promotes prevention through education.

The authors have enriched the field with a book that provides an understanding of the problem from the family dynamics to the classroom environment and finally to the overall culture of the school. Creative and thoughtful tools for intervening are provided, many of which have application beyond the school. Practitioners will benefit from the resource guide, the reading list, and the solution-focused techniques for building empathy and compassion in children.

The middle school and high school years are an ideal time for intervention: students are developmentally ready to conceptualize and deal with these issues; teachers and coaches are in optimal roles to influence adolescent peer groups in positive, healthy directions; and classroom discussion can be directed towards developing abstract thinking and idealism. These are the years that are most appropriate for moving from prevention efforts to a strong anti-bullying campaign. This handbook is an important addition to efforts across the country to create safe schools where bullying is not tolerated and caring, empathetic school atmospheres are valued.

Carla Garrity, Ph.D.
Kathryn Jens, Ph.D.
Bill Porter, Ph.D.
Nancy Sager, M.A.
Cam Short-Camilli, L.C.S.W.
Authors of *Bully Proofing Your School*

CHAPTER

AN OVERVIEW OF BULLYING

Boxer

Slightly overweight, sixth-grader Sara was new to the school district. The boys considered her homely. It did not help her self-image that she had developed breasts early and was awkward.

The boys called her "Boxer." She was a "dog" and would have no boyfriends. Even the other girls rejected her, as if her homeliness were catching.

The crueler boys did more than call her names. She was pinched; her breasts were poked. Students pushed her books to the floor. Ink blots appeared on her assignments. The abuse steadily increased.

The classroom teacher was quiet and likable but diffident. The more aggressive boys had taken unofficial, but effective, control. Sara first protested weakly, tearfully, then gave up, resigned to her status. She haunted the classroom with a stricken and fearful look. Sara had no confidence, no friends, and, seemingly, no future.

Sam

"Fat Sam, the Walking Encyclopedia." These words clearly meant that another prank was to be played: more knees would be skinned, more dignity— that precious and rare commodity for an eighth-grader—deducted from the already meager store. "Fat Sam, Fat Sam." The call was clear each morning on the school bus; it rang out at lunch when teachers' backs were turned.

An intelligent boy, Sam often wondered what pleasure it gave his classmates to ridicule him. In past years, he had lost his temper, had even been in a fight or two over the name calling. But the bigger boys had made two things clear. First, he was going to be Fat Sam forever whether he liked it or not. Second, any student who wanted to could call him that—the more aggressive young men would protect the few fellows less physically able than Sam. Sam put forward a convincing but false face of equanimity.

One day, Sam borrowed his father's nine-millimeter pistol and took it to school in a book bag. He must have thought about the gun all morning. Just after lunch, as students were settling into their fifth-hour English class, the call "Fat Sam" started up. Sam reached into the book bag and drew out the pistol. Two of the boys who had been taunting him for years died within seconds of one another. Seeming to emerge from a dream, Sam looked at the carnage, put the gun to his own head, and pulled the trigger.

Bullying, Aggression, and Violence

Our society has a legacy of aggression. We employ violence to resolve a host of problems, and we have done so since our nation's turbulent birth. Our frontier conquests and our relationship with indigenous people were steeped in violence. The fact that our national fabric, our way of being, is tied up in aggression can be seen in the alarming incidence of violence in our family relationships. Violence has become the norm in a variety of social contexts, and its results will be with us for at least the next generation.

From Violence to Schoolyard Bullying

This volume focuses on an insidious aspect of violence: the day-to-day teasing and harassment referred to as bullying (Olweus, 1978) or mobbing (Pikas, 1989a). Mobbing and bullying constitute a link between quasi-acceptable modes of coercive behavior and more clearly dangerous aggression.

Just because a school does not need metal detectors and police patrols, it does not mean that students find schools psychologically safe. In our investigations, 75% to 90% of students looking back over their school careers report that they suffered harassment at the hands of fellow students. As many as 15% of fourth through eighth-graders may be severely distressed by bullying (Hazler, Hoover, & Oliver, 1991; Hoover, Oliver, & Hazler, 1992; Hoover, Oliver, & Thomson, 1993). These samples were drawn from relatively homogenous, rural areas and small midwestern towns, areas that might be described as pleasantly pastoral. Nonetheless, these children suffer at the hands of their peers.

The best, most natural starting point for reducing aggression in schools is to reduce bullying. But how many schools effectively try to stem this interpersonal violence now and prevent its future growth?

This book provides a comprehensive tool for understanding, preventing, and reducing bullying. It contains a collection of effective nonviolent teaching and counseling models. These models are designed for use by all helping professionals who work in schools or who advise schools on disciplinary issues. Principals, counselors, school psychologists, and teachers will find the methods and activities outlined in these pages useful.

The procedures for dealing with bullying in Chapters Five through Nine are targeted toward middle school teachers, counselors, students, and the parents of these students. We found that bullying, though a problem in elementary schools, interfered with growth most during the period spanning fifth through eighth grades. In addition, some of the ideas slated for class discussions may not become cognitively accessible to students until they reach this age. However, many of the ideas in this book can be adapted for older or younger students.

Middle schools make an excellent target for anti-bullying efforts because of the developmental tasks that characterize this period. Adolescents and pre-adolescents, desiring to develop their own identities, look perhaps for the first time outside the home for support and seek answers about what to believe and how to behave. This search for autonomous identity often leads to ardent dependence on the peer group, which is the reason middle school students feel peer rejection and abuse so strongly. When young people first enter the extra-familial interpersonal world, they often are confronted with coercive and angry behavior from their peers. It is shameful that we do not do more to help them through what must seem to be a maze of interpersonal-relationship problems and questions.

Some readers may ask, "Why should we be dealing with schoolyard bullying? It is just a matter of 'boys being boys,' and it has gone on for ages." Perhaps it has, but that hardly justifies avoiding the problem. It is time to say that it will no longer be considered appropriate for an overweight boy, a homely girl, or a sensitive "musical" student to be held hostage to a social order enforced in schools by tough, troubled youth. Olweus (1991) argued that children in democratic societies bring their rights to school with them:

> *Every individual should have the right to be spared oppression and repeated, intentional humiliation, in school as in society at large* (p. 427).

Only recently have we come to understand the importance of schoolyard bullying. Olweus (1987) and Eron (1987) have shown that bullies identified by age eight are six times more likely to be convicted of a crime by the age of twenty-four and five times more likely than non-bullies to end up with serious criminal records by the age of thirty. Further, aggressive behavior is learned early and becomes resistant to change if it persists beyond eight years of age (Walker, 1993).

We must take bullying seriously and must not equate it with the normal "rough-and-tumble" of child development. Not only is bullying a precursor to greater and more dangerous violence, it also fosters intense misery among students.

There may have been a time when the honing of competitive and aggressive skills in rough play had survival value for the human species. Perhaps that is why bullying appears so natural to many young people (Hazler, Hoover, & Oliver, 1991; Oliver, Hoover, & Hazler, 1994). In our research, we often were struck by the degree to which young people saw bullying as part of the natural order of things. A lack of concern about bullying has also been noted among teachers in English secondary schools (Arora & Thompson, 1987). American high school students felt that teachers knew of their plight but were unwilling to intervene (Hazler, Hoover, & Oliver, 1991; 1992), perhaps another sign of the seemingly normative nature of bullying.

The following discussion of bullying begins with a definition of precisely what is meant by the term. We then place bullying within a theoretical framework. We are aware of the aversion that many practitioners (rightly) have for "mere" theorizing, and we will avoid this. However, it is important at the outset to develop a big picture, a context that will give structure and meaning to the available information.

We examine the belief system, the attitudes and ideology that support and maintain bullying among middle school students. Later, the causes of bullying will be examined, as will exemplary intervention efforts. The final chapters of this book will contain specific suggestions for reducing bullying in educational settings. Several chapters are dedicated to working with casualties—those students already caught up in the cycle of aggression either as victims or bullies.

Definition of Bullying

Currently, the most widely accepted definition used by writers and researchers is:

A person is being bullied or victimized when he or she is exposed, repeatedly and over time, to negative actions on the part of one or more persons (Olweus, 1991, p. 413).

"Negative actions" refers to the intentional infliction of, or attempt to inflict injury or humiliation, on another. The injury may be physical, such as an assault. Verbal attacks, with the aim of causing psychological discomfiture, are also included within the concept of bullying. Occasionally, bullying may comprise a mix of verbal and physical harassment. Verbal harassment may be employed to generate anger in weaker students so that the stronger individual has an excuse to initiate physical bullying.

Bullying is always directed by a stronger student against a weaker one. This can take many forms; for example, a physically stronger student could punch or kick a peer too physically weak to counterattack. A student higher on the social pecking order might verbally harass a lower-status student—even one who may be physically stronger—if social strata are rigid enough to restrain the victim from self-defense. Teasing is often directed from a more verbally facile student to one who is not so linguistically quick. In one study, we found that a majority of bullying was perpetrated by males, whether against males or females (see also

Olweus, 1991). Thus it is possible that teasing with a sexual content, which starts in the early elementary years, may be a precursor to sexual harassment in a society where females have a power disadvantage.

Several points need to be made in distinguishing bullying from other forms of aggression. First, bullying represents a chronic pattern of abuse over time, not individual or rare episodes. Second, bullying is not necessarily one-on-one harassment; it may be carried out by a group on a single individual. In this latter instance, it has been referred to as "mobbing" (Pikas, 1989a).

Bullying may involve either overt or covert actions. Olweus distinguished between "direct" and "indirect" bullying. Direct bullying involves open attacks on a victim, while indirect bullying is often covert in nature and frequently takes the form of social isolation and exclusion from a group. In our studies in the rural Midwest, social ostracism was the second most common form of bullying identified by female respondents (Hoover, Oliver, & Thomson, 1993). The interpretation of bullying behaviors by students will be explored in more detail in Chapter Two.

The Roots and Development of Bullying

Because bullying and aggression are related and because more is known about the development of aggression, the latter construct will be examined. Fortunately, there is a considerable history of empirical investigations from which to draw. Familial practices in early childhood are clearly associated with later antisocial and delinquent behavior. The preeminent authority in this area is Gerald Patterson of the Oregon Social Learning Center in Eugene. Patterson has conducted research into aggression and child-rearing practices for the past twenty-five years. He concluded that aggression is developmental in nature (see Fig. 1.1, Patterson, DeBaryshe, & Ramsey, 1989).

Figure 1.1. Developmental Progression for Antisocial Behavior

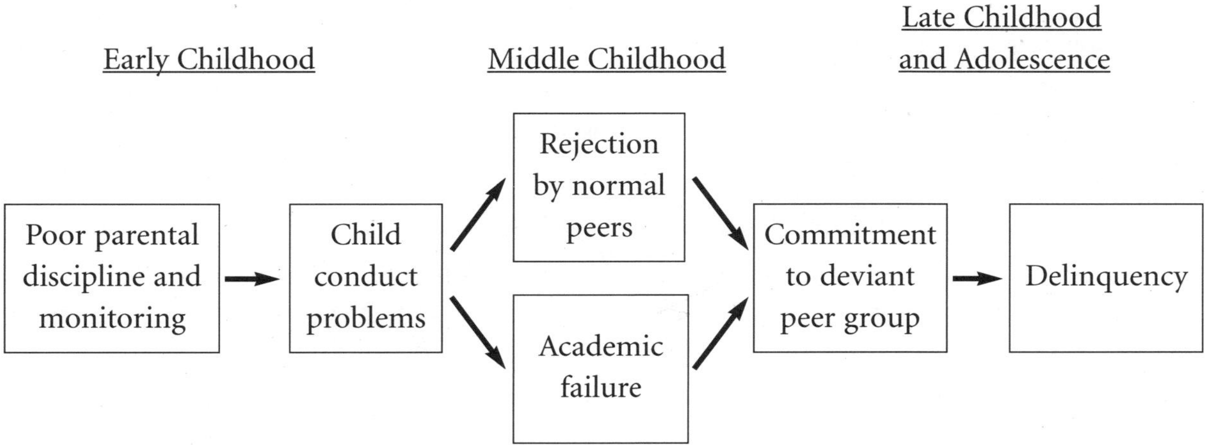

According to Patterson's research, child-rearing practices associated with the development of aggression include harsh and inconsistent disciplinary practices, limited parental involvement, and a lack of supervision. Similarly, Olweus (1991) characterizes the parenting received by many bullies as "too much freedom and too little love in the home environment" (p. 426). Schools and homes that lovingly set clear limits and boundaries and that are nurturing and caring probably prevent bullying. The specifics of these sustaining environments are examined in Chapter Six.

Some childhood aggression is instrumental in nature (Walker, Colvin, & Ramsey, 1995). That is to say, some children learn through rewards and punishments that they can get their needs met by attacking weaker peers. If a stronger boy procures a desired toy by attacking a playmate, he will be more likely to repeat the behavior in the future; this is particularly true in the absence of consequences. In addition, aggression clearly is associated with modeling; it can be learned by observing the aggression of others, particularly if those observed are seen receiving rewards for this behavior (Bandura & Walters, 1963).

As is depicted in Figure 1.1, early parenting practices lead to conduct problems by the time children reach grade school. By middle childhood, these problems among extremely aggressive children lead consistently to such outcomes as rejection by better-behaved peers and academic failure. In later childhood and adolescence, these behavior patterns may result in delinquency if the individual encounters a deviant peer group or receives the message in the home that antisocial behavior is accepted.

Some important comparisons between bullying and aggression deserve special mention. Early home environments of highly aggressive and mildly aggressive youngsters (a group that probably includes bullies) differ only in degree. This becomes readily apparent from an examination of the families of Scandinavian bullies (Olweus & Alsaker, 1991). These data point to an early family environment characterized by emotional coldness with spates of anger and, occasionally, outright verbal and physical aggression.

The child-rearing patterns noted by Olweus in the families of Scandinavian bullies bear a striking resemblance to motifs observed in the families of aggressive children. In short, we see an environment in which there are no constraints on the instrumental aggression that most children demonstrate at some point, or where only angry and coercive interaction patterns are modeled.

One highly significant qualitative difference has been observed between bullying and other forms of aggressive behavior. While problems of adult authority are common with bullies and some bullies may be labeled as conduct disordered, the behavior of bullies is seldom severe enough to lead automatically to peer rejection or academic failure. Olweus (1978), for example, found that bullies were as popular as a sample of so-called "well-adjusted" students, while chronic victims occupied the lowest rungs of the social ladder. The self-esteem of bullies tends to fall within the normal range, while this is not true of oppositional or other "externalizing" troubled youth.

We do not see bullying and aggression as synonymous, though they do share many features. Bullying may represent proto-aggression, which retains a degree of social respectability.

Bullying also shares features with such intergroup pressures as sexism and racism. In interviews with high school students, we found evidence that individuals with atypical gender behaviors were often singled out for abuse (see also Shakeshaft et al., 1995). Students may learn that it is acceptable to harass a member of their own racial, gender, or ethnic group who is somehow different. This kind of environment may be a petri dish in which intergroup hatred is cultured.

Both bullying and social discrimination are characterized by rituals. In the rite of submission, the bullying consists of forcing marked persons to perform detestable acts, by means of which power relationships are clearly enacted. Mihashi (1987) related an incident in which a physically weak student was marked with a felt-tipped pen and forced to dance in school hallways, with the result that he was transformed into a ridiculous sideshow. This dehumanizing ritual clearly communicated to the victim and others the subordinate and defenseless position that he or she was henceforth expected to occupy. In addition, bullying often entails a renaming rite, such as the use of "Fat Sam" noted earlier.

Finally, bullying often can be more than a psychological or group management issue. In many cases, bullying behaviors are illegal and dangerous. Increasingly, parents are seeking legal redress to the harassment of their children. The type of bullying directed toward young women often falls into the category of sexual harrassment (Shakeshaft et al., 1995). As such, it is illegal under Title IX of the Education Act. For example, a seven-year-old girl in Eden Prairie, Minnesota, successfully sought relief from sexually harassing remarks on the school bus (Sherer, 1993; Shoop, 1994). Increasingly, bullying prevention programs may be a necessity for schools given their *in loco parentis* legal responsibilities.

In the remainder of this book, we examine research on bullying in more depth and develop a model for reducing bullying in schools and communities. This model leads to several chapters that outline specific tactics for dealing with bully-victim problems. Specific methods include individual, group, and family counseling techniques; schoolwide anti-bullying information, and education-based campaigns. We include specific suggestions, based on our research, for evaluating the climate of schools for psychological safety.

Summary

- American schools exist in a larger culture steeped in violence and seemingly fascinated with aggression. While the exact relationship between bullying and aggression is unknown, the best guess is that bullying is an element of the pattern of antisocial behavior so troubling to citizens of the United States.

- Many of our nation's schools are neither the physically nor psychologically safe environments required by young people. School probably is experienced differently, depending on the vulnerability of individual students. But bullying is widespread, probably more troublesome than in years past. Up to 15% of students in ostensibly safe schools report themselves severely traumatized by peer abuse.

- Bullying is the physical or psychological harassment of persons less able to defend themselves than is the tormenter. It can involve only one tormentor or, in the case of "mobbing," many students can harass a lone individual.

- The best (but limited) evidence is that the families of bullies share fundamental characteristics with the families of aggressive children. Parents tend to be emotionally cold, hostile, and uninvolved. Bullying may be modeled after harsh discipline or physical abuse perpetrated in the home.

- As is true of aggression, some bullying may be instrumental; that is, it gets the bully what he or she desires or solves interpersonal social problems.

- To fully understand bullying, it is important to decipher the rituals involved, that is, the process of casting out those who are different by dehumanizing them, including the use of offensive names.

- Prevention of bullying may become a legal obligation of the schools.

CHAPTER 2

QUESTIONS AND ANSWERS ABOUT BULLYING

We must have information about bullying if we are to design effective programs to combat it. The following questions are frequently asked by educators and other helping professionals, particularly those with responsibilities for the physical and psychological health of children in schools and other educational facilities.

How prevalent is bullying?

The best way to measure the amount of bullying, at least as it is experienced by students, is to ask them directly. We did this in two studies in the rural Midwest, with astounding and troubling outcomes. In a sample of students from grades 8 to 12, roughly 80% of students responded that they had been bullied at some point in their school careers. Ninety percent of a younger sample (fourth through eighth-graders) also said they were victims (Hoover, Oliver, & Hazler, 1992; Hoover, Oliver, & Thomson, 1993).

Older students were asked to rate the severity of the bullying they received in five life areas or domains (familial, social, emotional, physical, and educational). We counted students as severely traumatized if they said they were severely traumatized by bullying in at least one life domain or were moderately bothered across all five domains. Fourteen percent of the older sample could be thus classified. We consider this to be a reasonable estimate of the proportion of students traumatized by bullying in rural, Midwestern schools.

The problem appears to be more severe in the U.S. than in any of the Western European countries, with the possible exception of Great Britain. Seven percent to 12% of secondary students from Norway were reported to be bothered "sometimes," a couple of times per week, or more often; the figure from Ireland is 8%, and 20.1% of English students reported that they were bullied (Smith, 1991).

We have begun to collect data from a national U.S. sample with methods similar to those employed in European studies. Preliminary analysis of information from randomly selected rural schools in one western U.S. state reveals rates somewhat higher than those from overseas. Eight percent of American students reported that they were bullied either once per week or more often. If students who reported that they were victimized "sometimes" are added to the previous categories, 20% of respondents had been harassed by peers "this year." Only 59% had not been bullied at some point during the survey year. Thus bullying appears to be more prevalent in the United States than in Europe, though U.S. estimates are comparable to those in England.

Midwestern students identified the junior high or middle school years as the worst ones for bullying. Peer harassment increased rapidly after grade 3 and diminished following grade 10. The overall highest rates of bullying and the most reported trauma resulting from it were during the middle school years, or approximately grades 5 through 8. This contrasts with European data, where bullying problems decrease nearly linearly after second grade and reach a low plateau at grade 7 (Olweus, 1991). American prevention programs should be targeted to grades 2–4. It is at this time that most individuals have developed the psychological acumen to understand human relations and where bullying may not yet be a severe problem. Anti-bullying campaigns seem best targeted to middle schools or junior highs.

In what life areas do students experience trauma?

Elementary, middle school, and high school respondents all experienced similar patterns of trauma from bullying. As might be expected, most students reported experiencing social and emotional disturbances. However, significant numbers (at least a fifth of each sample) evidenced problems in familial, academic, and physical life areas. Fourteen percent of the older sample (grades 8 to 12) reported that bullying diminished their ability to learn in school. Younger students reported academic difficulties at an even higher rate: 22% of fourth through eighth-graders reported academic difficulties resulting from peer abuse. Several anecdotal reports offered by students suggested that good grades and "egg-headedness" were a cause of the bullying they received in rural and small-town schools. Similar anti-intellectual peer pressures have been noted in major urban centers.

Significant gender differences were observed in the "emotional" domain in both studies. Females were distressed more often and were more emotionally troubled than were boys. Females' stronger affiliative needs at this age (Coleman, 1980) and males' reluctance to admit being traumatized may explain this gender difference. Nonetheless, it is important to note the consistency with which young women report themselves to be more troubled by peer rejection than are males. This matches what Mary Pipher (1994) wrote of the very difficult early adolescent period, when young women face what she termed "brutal" junior high school hallways. Female participants in a revealing study conducted by Shakeshaft et al. (1995) reported that bullying was devastating to their self-esteem and personal development. Several complained that only a very narrow range of behavior, dress, and conduct was allowed by elite students, and that the rest of the students were miserable much of the time.

What actions constitute bullying?

Young people describe bullying as predominately, though not completely, verbal behavior. The typical student troubled by bullying is much more likely to get verbal abuse, rather than a physical whipping. Nonetheless, young boys still report a great deal of physical bullying.

At all ages, students rated teasing as the most frequent bullying behavior. This was the case whether students were evaluating their own victimization (Hoover, Oliver, & Hazler, 1992; Hoover, Oliver, & Thomson, 1993) or were responding to observed abuse of others (Hazler, Hoover, & Oliver, 1991). Respondents clearly portrayed teasing under some circumstances as bullying. Shakeshaft et al. noted, "Verbal harassment was a part of the everyday fabric of school life" (1995, p. 37).

Perhaps the most intriguing finding to emerge from the midwestern studies was a sense of confusion among young people regarding the interpersonal dynamics of teasing. Students frequently expressed ambivalence about teasing; a common question was, "How do I know if my teasing is hurting someone?" Oliver, Hoover, & Hazler (1994) asked students to respond to the following statement: "Most teasing I saw was done in fun—that is, not done to hurt others." By an overwhelming margin (70.3%), older students endorsed this view; fully 90% of fourth through eighth-graders concurred. However, many of these respondents were the same individuals who rated teasing as bullying and who experienced associated trauma! Based on these results and our conversations with young people, we conclude that students hold conflicting attitudes about teasing. Some view it primarily as caustic harassment, others as playfulness. Many hold both views simultaneously, probably depending on the social context in which the teasing occurs.

Whether a verbal exchange constitutes bullying or whether it represents inclusive efforts at humor depends on many conflicting factors, including whether one is the teaser or the teased. First, whether an exchange represents teasing or playfulness may have to do with the social level or popularity of either the teaser or the one being mocked. If a student higher on the school's pecking order mocks a lower-status student, the exchange is likely to be seen by the latter student as status-affirming and thus an attack. Two individuals of equal rank may be able to partake in social banter as a sign of acceptance and familiarity. Second, verbal exchanges are likely to be complicated by the self-confidence of recipients. Third, the content of the interchange may predict how it is intended or received. For example, a male may see sexual innuendo as playful humor, while a female student may perceive the message as an attack. Fourth, the verbal acumen of students may affect their perceptions of teasing. More verbally able students may perceive teasing as harmless word play—without a great deal of literal meaning embedded in the dialogue. Less verbally facile individuals may hate to be teased—even playfully—because they deal with it poorly. Finally, personality probably plays a major role. Some individuals lack a sense of humor or perspective—and are seen by others as thin-skinned. Ironically, it is these students with low tolerance who often are foils for the jokes of others—because they respond to it viscerally.

While bullying is largely verbal in nature, there is more to it than that. Among younger males (grades 4–8), a considerable number reportedly received physical bullying, such as hits, kicks, and pokes (62% of bullied males, 55% of all males). Elementary and middle school females nominated ostracism as the second most common form of bullying after teasing (Hoover, Oliver, & Thomson, 1993). Bullying may foreshadow gender harassment and other between-groups disputes (Hoover & Juul, 1993). Teachers and students frequently express concern about how early verbal harassment contains sexual content (Shakeshaft et al., 1995). Shakeshaft and her colleagues noted that sexual harassment (poking breasts, other unwanted touching, sexual comments) was a frequent type of bullying received by females, particularly those whose physical development came early and whom others saw as attractive. Recent nationwide surveys reveal that many young women view junior high and middle school hallways as hostile gauntlets (American Association of University Women, 1993). No statistical relationship was found between bullying behaviors and the degree of trauma experienced. Teasing and other forms of verbal harassment are as potentially damaging to young people as occasional physical attacks.

What factors put students at risk for bullying?

Students in our survey were asked which behaviors put them or others at risk for peer harassment. Such a list may prove useful in targeting interventions to students at risk for becoming scapegoats. However, risk factors interact in complex ways with individual student personalities. Students who are psychologically healthy may not be traumatized, even if they display some risk factors. The social status of students may predict who will and will not be bullied. Olweus (1978) found that, among males, bullies were as popular as a comparison group of "well-adjusted" students; in contrast, chronic victims were rated as the most unpopular of the three groups. Similar values were expressed by the youth we interviewed in the Midwest. More than two-thirds of the female repondents agreed that bullies held higher social status than those who were "picked on" (Oliver, Hoover, & Hazler, 1994, p. 418). Nearly half of male respondents subscribed to this view.

Males and females of all ages selected the statement, "I [or they] just didn't fit in," as the most common reason for being bullied. Significantly, this rather nebulous item was added by students themselves when the survey form was piloted. It seems to be a generic statement about exclusion; more specific factors commonly selected by students are obvious examples of stigmata that may add to one's outsider status. Characteristics thought to be associated with bullying fell roughly into two categories—appearance and social status.

Common factors related to appearance are weight, weakness, and clothing. These were cited by both girls and boys. Girls frequently cited facial appearance. Social factors include such things as grades (either too high or too low) and who the victim's friends are. Figure 2.1 shows the five most common factors named by high school students and those selected most often by middle school students.

Figure 2.1: Highest Ranked Reasons for Being Bullied

A. Eighth through twelfth grade[1]

Rank	Males	Females
1	Didn't fit in	Didn't fit in
2	physical weakness	facial appearance
3	short tempered	cried/emotional
4	who friends were	overweight
5	clothing	good grades

B. Fourth through eighth grade[2]

Rank	Males	Females
1	didn't fit in	didn't fit in
2	who friends were	who friends were
3	physical weakness	clothes worn
4	short tempered	facial appearance
5	clothing	overweight

[1]Hoover, Oliver, & Hazler (1992)
[2]Hoover, Oliver, & Thomson (1993; data slightly reworked)

Students who answered our survey frequently volunteered information, particularly regarding perceived risk factors. Several female students wrote that they were abused by peers because of rumors that they were sexually promiscuous (Hazler, Hoover, & Oliver, 1991). Several students complained that they were bullied either because their behavior did not fit gender norms or because rumors had been spread that they were homosexual. During adolescence, sexual identity issues play a significant role in peer harassment. Gay bashing is frequently cited as a problem for teens (Hetrick & Martin, 1987). Shakeshaft and her colleagues argue that atypical gender-related behavior often triggers harassment of both males and females.

In interviewing and observing many middle and high school students, Shakeshaft and her colleagues found three distinct groups of students at risk for bullying. First, young women who were not seen as physically attractive were at risk for peer abuse. Second, males who did not fit the macho social image, those who were "artsy" or who did not enjoy athletics, frequently were bullied. Another at-risk group was females who developed early or who were seen as physically attractive by peers; these girls were sexually harassed.

The reasons that students give for being bullied do not seem to match reality. Other than physical weakness, no objective data point to clear social, behavioral, or physical differences between students who are bullied and those who are not (Olweus, 1991). Several possible reasons exist for the difference between objective information and student perceptions. First, the data showing no differences between victims and nonvictims were collected in Norway; it is possible that students in the United States are more demanding of normative dress, appearance, and behavior than are their Scandinavian counterparts. Second, if Olweus is correct and bullying is not elicited by victim characteristics, then there may be a degree of "blaming the victim," even self-blame, in students' desire to "explain" peer harassment in terms of personal attributes.

Which student attitudes support bullying?

In our sample of middle school children, more than 90% reported that they had been bullied. The magnitude of this response suggests that the degree of trauma experienced by bullied students does not deter some of them from harassing others, unless 10% of the students are bullying the other 90%, which is not a very likely prospect. In light of these findings, we questioned whether students agreed with statements that were supportive of bullying (Oliver, Hoover, & Hazler, 1994). Much to our astonishment, students readily endorsed several statements that supported peer harassment.

Both older and younger students agreed with the statement that victims brought it on themselves. More than 60% of the older sample endorsed this view, and a few students even felt that they were to blame for their own victimization (17% of males and 6% of females, Hoover, Oliver, & Thomson, 1993). Blaming the victim is a well-established psychological ploy for justifying oppression of one person by another.

Another 60% of students agreed that bullying actually helps students by making them tougher. This theme may explain why some adults may not be alarmed when confronted with bullying among young people. Perhaps, like the students we surveyed, many adults see bullying as part of the process of preparing students for the competitiveness of American society.

Another reason that one student may choose to bully another is that bullying is perceived as educative, that is, it "teaches about behavior unacceptable to the group" (Oliver, Hoover, & Hazler, 1994, p. 418). Males were much more likely than females to agree with this premise. Nearly half of male students (44.7%) agreed with the statement, compared with 30.0% of females. Almost twice as many boys *strongly* agreed that bullying teaches about unacceptable behavior than did females (15.2% vs. 8.3%). Unfortunately, nearly half of students (48.1%) agreed that befriending a scapegoat would result in reducing the Good Samaritan's social standing.

What can be done about bullying?

Based upon his bullying research, Olweus was asked by the Norwegian Ministry of Education to organize a nationwide anti-bullying campaign. The procedures used by Olweus and his team to combat bullying are easily adapted to the United States, and they are reviewed in Chapter Five. One conclusion reached in evaluating the Norwegian project was that educational efforts must be accompanied by clear standards and penalties for bullying behaviors.

Many curricula have been developed over the past decade to reduce violence in the schools. These anti-aggression curricula may be usefully employed as part of a schoolwide anti-bullying campaign. The curriculum most directly confronting bullying problems, *Bully Proofing Your School* (Garrity et al., 1995, p. 100), is an excellent guide that targets elementary children, though many of the activities are easily adapted for middle school. Other anti-bullying guides are available, notably the RECESS Program and a British anti-bullying program developed by Besay.

Other Activities

Many activities have been proposed as part of anti-bullying efforts. One common denominator in most of these endeavors is that they represent methods to encourage groups of antisocial students to interact in a prosocial manner. No research specifically supports the use of these procedures to reduce bullying. Nonetheless, they hold a great deal of promise.

For example, peer tutoring and cooperative learning have been used not only to increase the academic skills of slow learners but also to bring students with disabilities together with non-disabled peers (Ehly & Larson, 1980). Similarly, Perske and Perske (1988) proposed that non-disabled students serve as "circles of friends" for their counterparts with severe and multiple disabilities. These programs can be used to bring all students together. An ethic of caring, friendship, and shared community values may be an essential feature of bullying prevention projects.

Cooperative Education. Classrooms can be organized so that traditional, subject learning is accompanied by lessons in cooperation and group dynamics. Such activities have been shown to enhance learning, or at least not harm it, while improving cooperative skills and producing gains in the social inclusion of students with disabilities (Johnson & Johnson,

1994). It is likely that classrooms structured to foster greater inter-dependence may reduce bullying.

Victim-Offender Mediation. While training students in conflict resolution has been proposed as a way to reduce bullying (Maxwell, 1989), it may not be appropriate to rely on conflict resolution methods in situations where a clear perpetrator and victim exist, because it is unfair and potentially traumatizing for victims to deal with their abusers face to face. In such situations, victim-offender mediation may be a better alternative (Knowlton & Muhlhauser, 1994).

Victim-offender mediation procedures are similar to a counseling approach that targets specific bullying problems. Called the Common Concern Method, it is designed to help a group of bullies come to understand the scapegoat's dilemma and then to foster resolution plans on the part of all parties (Pikas, 1989b). This system is explored in more depth in Chapter Eight.

Summary

- Bullying is likely more problematic in the United States than in Europe. Roughly one in six students in rural schools considers him or herself traumatized by bullying. No gender differences in victimization rates were noted.

- Males perpetrate the most bullying, independently of victim sex.

- Bullying appears to be most problematic during the middle school or junior high years. This is true both in terms of sheer numbers of occurrences and the trauma reportedly experienced.

- Students report most disturbance in the social and emotional arenas, though a substantial minority reported being bothered in other life areas, including school learning.

- As portrayed by rural midwestern students, bullying appears to be largely verbal in nature, primarily comprised of teasing. Considerable physical bullying occurs among younger males, and female students were troubled by social ostracism.

- Students were ambivalent about teasing. On the one hand, they saw it as a form of bullying, and many reported it to be bothersome. On the other hand, a clear majority believed that it was generally done "in fun."

- Anti-bullying campaigns must include discussions of the topic of teasing and verbal harassment if they are to be successful.

- Students saw divergent behavior, dress, social comportment, or low social status as factors putting them at risk for peer abuse. It is not clear, however, that chronic scapegoats are objectively different from students not victimized.

- Students expressed ideas that could be portrayed as supportive of bullying. Many young people blamed the victim, felt that bullying could be educational for students with divergent lifestyles, and that bullies attained higher social status than did victims. Many also believed that by befriending a bullied person, one risked lowering one's own social status.

- Anti-bullying campaigns are needed in American schools, as bullying is a widespread problem that produces a significant degree of harm.

- A successful model has been developed and tested for reducing schoolyard bullying in Norway.

- Methods developed in other contexts, such as cooperative education and peer tutoring, may prove useful in American anti-bullying campaigns.

CHAPTER 3

A BULLYING INTERVENTION MODEL

Little excuse remains for not preventing and treating bullying in American schools. The school must protect the students' right to be safe while growing, learning, and developing. This chapter presents a model that educators can use to treat and prevent bullying. The remaining chapters expand this model and explore in more depth specific suggestions and procedures for the prevention and reduction of bullying and mobbing. The appendices reproduce the forms, interview questions, and checklists to be used in the program.

Although each component of the model is discussed separately, none can stand alone. Community and student involvement are necessary, as are an educative component and discussions of teasing involving educators and students. However, each school will face specific circumstances, particularly regarding the severity of bullying and the availability of resources, that will require the school to emphasize selected aspects of the anti-bullying program.

Practitioners can employ the model as part of a lobbying effort to generate needed resources. For example, evaluation may reveal that a need exists to hire or train a school counselor with sufficient expertise to perform the individual or group counseling activities. Administrators may decide that it is wise to release educators for curriculum research and development as bullying prevention activities are planned.

The primary elements of this program are necessary precursors to a safe school. The degree to which school officials can undertake these activities may vary, but they must be present in some form for a school to be even potentially psychologically safe. In addition, these entities are necessary precursors to more intensive and individualized services. These global underpinnings of the anti-bullying school are described briefly below. In a similar vein, Prothrow-Stith (1994) has described a public health, community-wide approach to teaching nonviolence.

Bullying is unacceptable. There is schoolwide agreement on disciplinary standards.

Based on his pioneering work in bullying treatment and prevention, Olweus concluded that good intentions do not solve bullying problems. In coordination with parents and students, middle school personnel must set and enforce behavioral standards regarding the unacceptability of bullying.

Most school discipline codes include prohibitions of physical attacks. Relatively few schools, however, have speech codes to protect the rights of students against humiliation. While speech codes can be troublesome because they might conflict with rights of free speech, a dialogue about the rights of students to be free from verbal abuse must take place.

Clarity regarding the unacceptability of school bullying and rules prohibiting the purposeful humiliation of others are necessary, but by themselves they are not sufficient to prevent bullying. In addition, even if these rules are in place, educators should reexamine them regularly in light of peer victimization problems that arise. Walker, Colvin, & Ramsey (1995) provide a superior overview of the best practices for developing a schoolwide, proactive discipline program.

The Empathetic School

The notion of being "my brother's keeper" must permeate a school before students will deal ethically with one another, particularly with weaker members of the group. Teaching about interdependence and the worth of individuals must fill the school. These issues ought to be raised in the context of a schoolwide information campaign. While the information program may begin with one-shot inservices, workshops, and student programs, it must be continued in each room.

The Anti-Bullying Information Campaign

Specific information about bullying and its consequences are essential to the mental health of middle and junior high school. Getting the anti-bullying message out was a central feature of the successful campaign undertaken by Dan Olweus (1991) on behalf of the Norwegian Ministry of Education. An anti-bullying educational campaign is discussed in Chapter Four.

Referral Mechanism

The foundational activities listed above should greatly enhance the quality of life in most schools. However, many problems brought to the school by students are relatively intractable. Thus a mechanism must be in place for bringing students to the attention of helping professionals inside and outside the school.

An excellent starting point for the referral mechanism is the evaluation activities discussed in Chapter Five. In addition, the risk factors discussed in Chapter Two may serve as warning signs for counselors and teachers as they seek students whose quality of life may be under pressure from peer abuse. For the referral mechanism to work, a climate must be established in which students are not afraid to admit that they hurt, are confident that hurting students are taken seriously in the school, and are willing to present themselves for treatment and help.

The above methods are largely preventative in nature. Those that follow are more therapeutic in orientation.

Group and Individual Psychotherapy

Methods have been developed for working with individual bullies and victims. These include the Common Concern Method proposed by Pikas (1989b), which is designed to lessen the impact of bullying on school-age children. This method, which is described in Chapter Seven, helps mobbers to understand the feelings of victims and helps all involved parties to agree on a solution. The cognitive retraining of both victims and bullies also is proposed as a treatment modality. In addition, such methods as daily reports, contingency contracting, and self-monitoring are explored in Chapter Eight.

Family-Based Approaches

Generally, the families of bullies are characterized by excessively loose structure, a cool to cold emotional climate, and a lack of supervision. This cold, unsupervised, or actively hostile environment appears to contribute to both aggression and bullying. In contrast, many families of chronic scapegoats appear to be over-involved and highly overprotective. To deal effectively with bullying, the program must address the family dynamics of both the bullies and the chronic victims.

Bibliotherapy and Coping Strategies

Many fiction writers have broached the topic of schoolyard bullying. Teachers and counselors can use this literature to introduce the topic of bullying and to initiate discussions of possible solutions. This can be employed with individual victims and bullies or can be a general approach to bullying as a class-wide topic in literature or social studies. Bibliotherapeutic information is reviewed in Chapter Seven.

Referrals to Mental Health Agencies

While an integrated system, such as the one proposed here, has a good chance of preventing and treating most mild child-on-child aggression, it is important to note that in any school there are severely troubled children, particularly those from extremely abusive backgrounds and those suffering from more substantial mental health problems. Thus it is important for school officials to have a well-established system for recognizing troubled children and referring them to mental health and special education authorities.

This latter point about a referral system is not trivial and cannot be left to chance. For example, it is known that far more children experience mental health problems than ever receive therapy or services in American schools. Rubin and Balow (1978), for example, found that approximately 7% of randomly selected students in Minnesota schools were identified by every teacher between kindergarten and fifth grade as exhibiting mental health problems that interfered with learning, yet in no single year have more than 1% of students been served as behaviorally disordered. This state of affairs cannot continue if children are to be saved from the severe problems they suffer. An important aspect of a "quality of life" orientation by school personnel, then, is advocating for appropriate services for children.

Summary

- A global model for the treatment and prevention of bullying was laid out. The model uses an umbrella to represent shelter from the storm experienced by many of our youth.

- An anti-bullying campaign, much in the model of that undertaken by the Norwegian Ministry of Education, is one feature of a global anti-bullying campaign.

- It is important that schools set and enforce discipline standards if they are to lessen the impact of bullying within their walls.

- The ambience of schools must be one in which each individual is valued and an ethic of interdependence is taught.

- The Common Concern Method (Pikas, 1989b) is a model for helping bullies understand the impact of bullying on individual victims.

- General individual psychotherapeutic techniques may be applicable, with some modification, to the problem of bullying. Such methods are developed in this book.

- Cognitive retraining procedures may be fruitful in getting victims and bullies to therapeutically "re-think" and reinterpret environmental events.

- Contingency contracting and self-monitoring are methods that may have useful anti-bullying applications.

- Mechanisms must be in place in schools to direct the problems of more severely involved students to the proper mental health agencies.

CHAPTER

4

ASSESSMENT AND EVALUATION: HOW IS YOUR PROGRAM DOING?

As educators work to reduce bullying and engender a friendlier environment for learning and growing, they require information about how best to direct the program. In addition, administrators need information about the effectiveness of anti-bullying efforts as well as information about how well specific features of the program worked and how these features added to the overall effect. In short, evaluation is a central component of an effective anti-bullying campaign. This chapter provides suggestions for evaluating the anti-bullying campaign. Their degree of specificity is based on the degree to which information from research is currently available; more research equals more specific program-evaluation standards.

Formative and Summative Evaluation

Evaluation information can be either summative or formative. Summative evaluation is used to judge the results of a program, demonstrating the degree to which it worked. Summative evaluation techniques answer the following questions: Was the program successful in decreasing bullying or its impact on students? How much was bullying decreased? Which specific bullying behaviors were reduced? Were students aware of the anti-mobbing efforts, and did they value the various activities that were organized around this theme?

Formative evaluations are used to fine-tune the program as it is in progress. For example, it might be found that the program seems to be more effective with females than with males. If this is the case, anti-bullying efforts can be altered to reach males. Or counseling efforts may prove to be more effective than information campaigns. In such a case, more time and effort may be dedicated to providing counseling services and less to instruction, or, alternatively, the information campaign may be strengthened.

The data collection instruments and techniques outlined here can be used to evaluate outcomes of a variety of schoolwide disciplinary programs, not just the anti-bullying efforts that are the theme of this book. Where possible, comparative data from the Midwest bully studies are provided. We ask that users of this manual send the results of their studies to us care of National Educational Service so that we can provide more useful norms for the bullying climate (an address is provided on page ii). The questionnaires and interviews in the appendices may be reproduced by purchasers of this book.

Tools

Several instruments were developed so that educators could have a starting point for evaluating bullying problems in their schools. These instruments are also designed to facilitate the evaluation of anti-bullying programs.

For the most part, ideas for the questionnaires flow from studies conducted in the rural, upper Midwest from 1990 to 1993 (Hazler, Hoover, & Oliver, 1991; Hoover, Oliver, & Hazler, 1992; Hoover, Oliver, & Thomson, 1993). In addition, the instruments were altered to take into account the data from Olweus's methods developed in the Scandinavian countries and variations on this body of work undertaken by, among others, Smith (1991) in Great Britain. Every attempt has been made in the development of these tools to make them accessible to fourth through eighth-grade students. However, where reading levels are generally low, the responses using Likert or level-style formats should be changed to ones with a simple yes-or-no rubric (see Hoover et al., 1993). The evaluator may read items to students with disabilities, provided that confidentiality can be assured and the reader is trusted by the respondent.

The surveys and interview questions designed for evaluating the anti-bullying program outlined here are included as appendices to this book. They may be reproduced by purchasers of *The Bullying Prevention Handbook* and modified as seen fit by users. Each survey or interview format is described briefly below.

Form B (pp. 109–113)

Form B was designed to easily provide summative pre and post-intervention information. It contains items drawn largely from the midwestern bully studies described in Chapter Two. It contains items that measure student demographics, the frequency of harassment, bullying behaviors, and dangerous locations in the school. Students are requested to evaluate efforts to reduce interpersonal friction in the setting and rate the quality of the school's responses to bullying. Finally, students are asked about attitudes toward bullying.

Form P (pp. 114–116)

Form P was designed as either an alternative to Form B or a companion instrument. Form P is intended to better assess the process, rather than the result, and to reflect changes in attitudes and actions regarding harassment. In some respects, Form B can be thought of as a summative document, while Form P is designed more for formative evaluation. We recommend that officials randomly assign each form to half of the evaluation sample.

Items on Form P relate to the specific nature of activities undertaken in the program. For example, items 1 to 7 in Part A ask how often bullying topics have been raised in classes. Part B deals with the quality of discussions about bullying topics such as getting along, teasing, and gender relationships. Note that these questions are appropriate for use during the pretest or fall evaluation period (see schedule below). Questions about process are important during a baseline period for two reasons. First, it is not impossible that activities of this nature are already being undertaken and that students value them. In this case, anti-bullying programming may consist of tightening or expanding activities that already exist. Second, if few such activities are occurring, the first administration of Form P will provide a useful yardstick against which to judge new programming. Of course, the most useful aspects of Form P will be manifested during the second and subsequent years of the program. This is because activities can be honed based on student reactions to them.

Suggested Interview Questions (pp. 117–118)

While Form P is designed to assess the process of the bullying reduction and prevention program, an even deeper source of information may be elicited by empaneling a group of students. Then, on a pre/post basis, practitioners pose both the closed and open-ended questions, or a subset of them.

These questions were constructed with two purposes in mind. First, they are worded to maximize student responses. Of course, the responsiveness of members of the panel, or even individual students interviewed in isolation, depends on the expertise of interviewers. It would be beneficial to employ staff trained in interview methods to conduct the interviews with students, as the issues raised during these sessions are likely to be sensitive. Counselors, school psychologists, and social workers often receive this training as part of their preservice programs. Another possibility would be to bring in an outside evaluation specialist. Most colleges and universities maintain research units staffed with experts in qualitative evaluation, interviewing, and research techniques. Such individuals would be particularly valuable when analyses are completed.

A second purpose of the questions is to delve deeper into the same issues raised by survey instruments. Open-ended interviews often produce richer, more nuanced types of information. This may be the most useful data for setting agendas and monitoring the anti-bullying process. With this in mind, we recommend that interviews be collected from the same students during each data-collection period. As mentioned above, evaluation team members can decide whether to use a focus group, to interview students individually, or to employ some combination of these methods.

Student Evaluation of Counseling Services (pp. 119–120)

Feedback forms were developed for use in evaluating such activities as group and individual counseling sessions. (Descriptions of effective practices in these domains are described in Chapters Six, Seven, and Eight.) If referrals for youth troubled by bullying lead to sessions with specially trained helping professionals, the evaluation form on pages 119–120 may prove useful in documenting satisfaction with these efforts or revealing grounds for improvement during Year Two. Obviously, if counseling practices do not specifically target bullying prior to initiation of the campaign, no pretest evaluation data can be collected with this format.

Other Procedures

Several other procedures are recommended for an effective anti-bullying campaign. These materials are not provided here for two reasons. First, some of the methods recommended below should already be in place. Second, many of them will be idiosyncratic to the specific menu of anti-bullying activities. For example, it would be very difficult to predict ahead of time which materials will be employed in schools to provide information to students. Thus evaluations of whether this information was learned will have to be targeted specifically to the concepts stressed in a program.

Didactic Tests. Teachers or counselors should develop evaluations of knowledge of the conceptual material introduced. This information would be helpful in determining how clearly students learned the content of anti-bullying information.

Incident/Behavioral Reports. Most states require that incident reports be filled out, collected, and filed. This documentation is designed to keep track of serious institutional behavioral occurrences. It is important to formalize this process—perhaps going so far as to provide inservice training to practitioners so that reports are filled out in a standardized manner. If this is done, resulting data could be tracked for responsiveness to the anti-bullying program. Olweus (1991) found that anti-bullying efforts also decreased other antisocial behavior such as fights and vandalism. Carefully crafted incident reports would be a sensible way to track these ancillary behaviors.

Attendance and Tardy Records. Chronic victims of peer abuse miss more school than other students (Lee, 1993). Thus attendance records might be another source of information regarding the effectiveness of a schoolwide anti-bullying campaign. Likewise, a healthier school might engender a lower incidence of tardiness, because the status of being late can represent an avoidance response. If such information is to be helpful in gauging the effectiveness of a program, care must be taken to standardize the collection of information. This will allow clearer inferences to be made regarding the effects of policy and educational efforts to reduce bullying.

Journals. Students and teachers can be encouraged to keep journals dedicated to interpersonal relationships and related topics. If they are willing to share them, these journals may be very helpful in developing the "story" of the anti-bullying campaign and its impact on individuals. Recommendations for the use of journals are listed in Chapter Eight.

Academic Performance. The overall psychological climate of a school is related to academic achievement (Anderson, 1982). As a result, schoolwide reductions in bullying may produce small but measurable improvements in achievement. Of course, the effect would likely be most noticeable if evaluators analyzed the performance of victimized students separately.

Group-administered testing from the year before an anti-bullying campaign begins could be compared with the next fall's performance as an indicator of academic outcomes of anti-bullying efforts. Since the effect is likely to be small, a lack of overall improvement does not indicate failure of the program, nor can improvements necessarily be attributed to the anti-bullying campaign. Academic achievement, combined with other measures, may, however, add to the evidence for or against gains based on the project.

Timetable

For the sake of simplicity, a timetable is assumed where anti-bullying efforts are undertaken early in the fall, following a meticulous planning period in the summer. The evaluation procedures described here will follow this timetable, though they certainly can be altered in light of the local situation.

Summer

During the summer months, several tasks related to evaluation of anti-bullying efforts must be completed as part of the planning process. First, forms must be reproduced in sufficient numbers to collect relevant information. Second, it is important to generate accurate and complete course and student lists in order to have these materials ready for sampling procedures. Finally, a sequence of evaluation activities must be planned well ahead of time so that such efforts do not conflict with the busy opening weeks of the school year and the initiation of the anti-bullying campaign. Most likely, evaluation planning and organization of the overall bully reduction plan will be undertaken simultaneously. It is probably a good idea to form a subcommittee with responsibility primarily for evaluation.

Sampling approximately 15% of the student body is recommended on both a pre and post basis. Certain sampling frames must be filled in order to ensure representation of all pertinent groups; this may be done most simply by sampling multi-age classes. If too few multi-grade classes occur in a given school, then "teachers" can serve as the sampling unit, and the students of 15% of the teachers in the building can be sampled.

It is unlikely that reasonably accurate information will be forthcoming from students if names are collected. However, it has been shown that, given strict adherence to confidentiality, student self-report information is nearly as accurate as more objective observational data (Olweus, 1991). The most accurate information will result from pre/post assessment of the same students. To do this, a list must be kept of students' names associated with index numbers on surveys. Students must be reassured that, following the evaluation cycle, the list of names will be destroyed so that no one will be able to identify a student's responses.

If, in the best judgment of school officials, the above system will stifle student response because names are collected, *separate* samples can be collected at pre and post-evaluation periods. While not as powerful a technique, the latter system should still reveal improvements, given that both samples are collected randomly. Note that, by chance, a few students will be in both pre and post groups.

Advanced techniques, such as stratified sampling, may be used if team members want to ascertain whether selected groups, such as minorities who are at risk for bullying, are represented in the sample. In this case, lists are made separately for each group to be represented, and the sample is drawn from these lists. No technical reason exists that smaller groups should not be over-represented on a proportional basis. For example, enough members of a minority group that is particularly at risk for being bullied must be sampled so that reasonable decisions can be made. Several excellent texts on research methods and program evaluation are available to guide the construction of samples.

The recommendation for 15% sampling is for medium-sized schools (from 500 to about 1,000 students). For smaller schools, a census of the entire student body may be in order. Serviceable information may be generated with smaller sample proportions from larger schools. It should be noted that, given random selection, it is possible that a small percentage of students will be selected two or even three times. This is not a problem. Nor will it greatly damage the representativeness of the sample if students are excluded from more than one panel.

Parents should be informed about both the anti-bullying campaign and the nature of the information to be collected. Where local district policy requires it, informed consent should be acquired from parents of students participating in the evaluation study; this could be completed during the summer months for the fall sample.

Fall

Data should be gathered no sooner than a month into the start of the school year. This is important because the questions are phrased in terms of the month preceding administration of the instrument. This time period was selected for several reasons. First, Olweus (1991; Olweus & Alsaker, 1991) points out that it is important to provide students with a meaningful time frame. Olweus used the "school term" as his unit of analysis, but this time period is too long to allow for pre and post-evaluations over one school year. The period of one week is a possibility, but the number of students bullied over one week will be so low that it may cause some members of the staff and public to conclude erroneously that bullying is not a problem. Because the instrument will become normative in subsequent years, the number of bullying episodes per month may be made an even more useful measure. However, the pre/post information for each school is most important for understanding the effects of anti-bullying campaigns, and that does not require normative data. The pre-test, in effect, becomes the norm against which post-test measures are judged.

Data are best collected before the start of the program. If this is not feasible, then survey forms should be collected as early in the program as possible. In cases where pre-test data are collected while the program is in progress, the effectiveness of anti-bullying efforts will be slightly underestimated. Forms P and B each are administered to half of the sample. Interview questions are administered either individually or in focus groups of approximately 10 to 15 students. The focus group should represent important constituencies in the building.

Midyear

Instruments could be readministered midyear to provide formative evaluation. Suggestions for fine-tuning efforts based on mid-year evaluations are provided below. The mid-year evaluation is not necessary, but it is recommended.

Spring

Toward the end of the school year, the data-collection procedures used in the fall are repeated. We recommend late April or early May as a sensible target for initiation of year-end evaluation procedures. After information is collected and analyzed, the anti-bullying team meets in order to answer the evaluation questions and to plan Year Two of the anti-bullying campaign.

Analysis: Evaluation Questions and Answers

Several issues in the evaluation of anti-bullying efforts are specifically addressed by the instruments and methods described in this chapter. The major evaluation questions are provided below as subject headings, followed by methods for considering formative and summative responses to each item.

Starting Out: Defining Issues

If the decision is made to undertake only a portion of the schoolwide program described in Chapter Three, rather than the entire plan, the specific approaches to be used may be determined by information from the fall pre-test. For example, if students identify specific locations in the school where they feel particularly vulnerable to being abused, then planners may wish to reallocate supervisory personnel to high-risk areas, even though that was not part of the program as originally planned.

Another possibility is that certain ideological issues arise from the "Attitudes about Bullying" section of Form B. An example would be where not many students blame the victim (#2) but where students embrace the notion that "bullying helps people by making them tougher" (#4). The discussions planned for classes or schoolwide anti-bullying efforts would reflect the attitudes expressed in the pre-test.

It is very important to work through initial interviews and Form P to determine students' common concerns. For example, it is quite possible that activities are already occurring that students see as fostering prosocial behavior in the school. These activities could be strengthened and continued, rather than allocating resources to new programs. The list of themes to watch for, presented below, derives from our experience talking to students, teachers, and counselors.

1. Gender relationships in the program. It is possible that special efforts may be necessary in order to make a setting as friendly to females as possible.

2. It is important to look carefully at data regarding vulnerability to peer victimization (Form P). Helping professionals can use this information to be alert to the characteristics of students who may be especially at risk for abuse.

3. Interview and Form P data may suggest that interracial relationships deserve attention.

4. Practitioners may discover that one key to reducing harassment in the setting is dealing with student-determined groups, such as "jocks," "nerds," and "heads," or even gangs.

5. To some extent, programs may be based on the sheer number of bullied students. For example, if more than 80% of students report that they have been bullied, increased time and resources may be required.

6. Teasing has proved to be a confusing and controversial topic. Examination of teasing items may reveal that the topic deserves particular attention. Young people may benefit from a discussion of such topics as when humor is hurtful, how to read others' body language, and related topics.

7. Look for the possibility that academic issues engender aggression. In some schools where a high achievement motivation exists, students who have trouble learning may be at risk. In other buildings, students who are oriented toward academics, the arts, or away from sports may be targeted (Shakeshaft et al., 1995).

It is important that topics of interpersonal concerns be allowed to emerge from students. The primary requirement for adults charged with evaluation is to be objective. In each setting, singular issues of concern will be identified. Many of these issues will cause concern to compassionate adults, and there may be an understandable tendency to want to sweep these issues under the rug. However, ignoring them will not make them disappear. An open-minded, observant look at initial data is the best way to design a meaningful program for each facility.

Evaluation of Psychotherapeutic Interventions and Other Activities

Forms B and P are provided in the appendices for evaluating the counseling process. The purpose is to determine whether students receiving specialized help—for example, by the "Common Concerns" approach—perceive that help as useful and worthwhile. These reaction forms can also be used to track the number of visits, which may be useful in documenting whether services are being delivered to troubled students. Of course, counselors may interpret these data with a grain of salt—particularly in instances where bullies have been brought into sessions somewhat unwillingly. However, the general tone of the information may help counselors to detect problems and strengths in the system.

Analysis of Evaluation Questions

What is the prevalence of bullying in our school? Several levels of analysis are available for answering this question. First, the percentage of students who answer "Yes" to the question of whether they have ever been bullied may be used in a broad sense to get a feel for the severity in the district, assuming that most students have been in the schools for a long period. At the pre-test, it will not be uncommon for half or more of the students to answer yes to that question. In the Midwest bully studies, 80% of high school students and 90% of middle-schoolers responded that they had been bullied during their school careers. When the pre-test information is compared to the spring evaluation, a significant reduction in the percentage of "Yes" answers broadly indicates the degree of improvement.

Indications of the degree of students experiencing bullying behaviors will provide a picture of bullying actions in the school (Form B, section B, Nos. 4–10). Mean item values can be calculated within groups by adding up the response scores and dividing by the number of students in the group. This procedure will allow inferences to be made about the "style" of bullying in the school—whether some groups receive bullying that is qualitatively different from the bullying perpetrated on others—and will set a baseline against which improvements may be judged.

Have we met our goals? After fall information is gathered, it is recommended that specific goals for the reduction of bullying be set, based on available data. One summative question is whether these goals have been met. The most sensible way to answer this question, of course, is to compare pre and post-testing data from the summative instrument (Form B). Even if goals have not been met, statistically significant reductions in rates of bullying, in mean "traumatization" values, and even in ratings of the number of bullying behaviors can be taken as evidence that the program is changing the school's or institution's climate.

The number of statistical tests that are done will add to the possibility of finding positive changes by "lucky chance," so the evaluation team should stick to their most pressing issues. Data should be analyzed item by item. Mean values by item can be generated by adding instances within items and then dividing by the number of cases.

Mean scores can be compared with parametric techniques. However, because of the current lack of information regarding the measurement properties of these instruments, evaluators may not be comfortable with this approach. Thus the data can be examined with nonparametric tests, such as chi square, to determine whether students tended to select a different pattern of responses after experiencing the anti-bullying program than they did in the fall assessment.

Even if parametric methods are employed, responses should not be averaged across items, because the instrument is not developed enough for its scaling properties to be established. On the first nine items (prevalence and bully behavior items), the desired direction of change is toward lower values, because lower values are associated with fewer episodes of bullying and fewer specific types of attacks.

Unfortunately, the forms included in this book are adapted from those used in research, and the degree of change that would indicate a desirable—or even possible—reduction in bullying behavior is not known. However, statistically significant reductions in several of the items would reflect substantial progress. In addition, an "effect size" can be calculated. This statistic allows evaluators to estimate reductions of bullying in standard deviation units (or what statisticians call z scores). Over a year, reductions by one standard deviation or more (based on pre-test values) would represent a very successful program.

Data that are collected constantly, such as incident reports and tardies, should be averaged by month and plotted graphically. If the bullying campaign is having an effect on these ancillary behaviors, a noticeable downward trend should be visible. If incident reports are available from past years, it would be wise to generate month-by-month reports for comparison purposes. These reports may reveal whether time-based trends occurred and whether current trends diverge from past behavior in the appropriate direction. Statistical methods are available for characterizing time and trend data.

Who Does the Bullying?

This question can be answered by examining results from item C, numbers 1 and 2, Form B. The two items deal with the gender of bullies and the age of bullies. Evaluators are looking for such patterns as boys consistently picking on girls or older students victimizing younger ones. Pre-to-post changes in the two items should be sensitive to positive changes induced by the bullying prevention program. Several interview items could be used to gain insight into tensions in the building, where bullies from one identifiable group appear to be victimizing others.

How do students perceive the performance of adults in the building? Young people are asked to rate the performance of school personnel in dealing with bullying in items C-1 through C-6, Form B. In addition, most items of the process version (Form P) also deal with this issue but from a pedagogical perspective. That is, students are asked whether adults in the facility are teaching and talking about bullying and interpersonal relationships.

These questions should allow for tentative judgments about how effectively adults intervene. As is true of other items, it is expected that more students will select favorable choices after the program has been in place for a school year.

Where is bullying occurring? Perhaps one of the most important sets of items for the pre-test period are those directed toward identifying "hot" spots in the building (Form B, Part D, items 1–9). The same question also can be posed during interviews. Raising the location issue allows administrators to pinpoint risky sites for adult supervision. Olweus (1991) lists this as an essential component of effective prevention programs.

Each area in the building should be assigned a score. This value is generated by assigning a point every time a student mentions that location. The higher the location score, the more bullying is occurring there.

What do students believe about bullying? The items on the last page of Form B are designed to examine student attitudes regarding peer harassment. Items were selected from the Oliver et al. study (1994) and should reveal troubling attitudes and issues that can be addressed during class discussions. These items will most likely show a decrease from pre to post-test as a function of quality programming and thus may serve as another summative indicator. However, these items, or ones like them, have never been employed in this manner.

Summary

Evaluation is an essential component of any schoolwide disciplinary program, including bullying prevention and treatment models. To develop the most effective program possible, educators should use both summative and formative evaluations. This book includes instruments for both purposes, including two survey instruments based on extant research literature, evaluation interview questions, and forms for documenting student satisfaction with counseling-type interventions.

Data collected in the fall should be carefully examined in order to provide direction for the anti-bullying program. Gender issues, informal student groupings, and attitudinal issues deserve special attention during the planning phase. These data can be compared to that from spring evaluations to show any reductions in bullying.

Summary

- Evaluation is an essential component of any schoolwide disciplinary program. The same is probably true of bullying prevention and treatment models.

- Summative evaluation refers to studies of outcomes from which a "yes or no" response to an evaluation question can be generated.

- Formative evaluation consists of the practice of collecting data that allows a program to be fine-tuned as it is in progress. Formative evaluation can be said to be evaluation of process.

- Two survey instruments based on extant research literature were developed.

- Evaluation interview questions and forms for documenting student satisfaction with counseling-type interventions were developed.

- Data collected in the fall should be carefully examined in order to provide direction for the anti-bullying program. Gender issues, informal student groupings, and attitudinal issues deserve special attention during the planning phase.

- Reductions in bullying can be detected by comparing pre-test to post-test scores, largely employing Form B. These data can also be derived from the process-type questions provided on Form P and from interview questions.

36

CHAPTER

5

A SCHOOLWIDE ANTI-BULLYING EDUCATION PROGRAM

The bare bones of an information campaign are given in this chapter. Concerned educators should refer to the resources mentioned here. Many of the ideas included in this chapter were generated by Dr. Olweus in his ground-breaking studies in Sweden and Norway. We especially refer readers to the Norwegian Ministry of Education anti-bullying campaign led by Olweus and his colleagues. Olweus himself developed a set of materials in English based on the Ministry of Education program. Such topics as the extent of bullying, familial background of bullies, and intervention methods are discussed. Many of these outcome papers were reviewed in the intervention section of Chapter Two (Olweus, 1978; 1984; 1991; Olweus & Alsaker, 1991).

Readers also are directed to an excellent volume, *Bully Proofing Your School* (Garrity et al., 1995). Many of the activities, information, and materials provided in *Bully Proofing* can easily be modified for middle school students. In fact, many of them are most appropriate for such individuals.

A compendium of bullying-related materials, along with available addresses, is provided in the appendices (pp. 145–148). Many of these materials can be used to flesh out the system proposed in these pages.

The Basics

Every social gain is initiated with the vision of a leader. In the case of an anti-bullying campaign, a concerned parent, teacher, student, or administrator must emerge with both an understanding that bullying is a problem and a mental picture of what an improved school would be like. This individual may have to work very hard to convince people that bullying is worth dealing with.

Many adults actively resist anti-bullying campaigns, for some quite understandable reasons. First, school or program officials may not want to admit that bullying is a problem out of a fear of raising a controversial issue. Some may see the issue as a challenge to their authority, professional skills, or parenting. A segment of the adult population views bullying as hopeless and believes that nothing can be done about it. Finally, some may portray bullying as a natural part of the social order that hones beneficial competitive and aggressive instincts.

All we can say to the concerned reader of this book is to keep plugging. Use the data presented in Chapters One and Two to convince other concerned parents or helping professionals that peer abuse is very damaging and that it can be reduced. Further, we need to keep reminding ourselves of the Norwegian experience: bullying prevention programs reduced many other undesirable behaviors in addition to peer harassment.

A Bullying Prevention Committee

The process of envisioning goals and setting an anti-violence agenda must be passed on from an initial visionary to an association of concerned persons. This committee should represent all constituencies affected by the campaign. Parents, teachers, students, and administrators, at minimum, must participate in the anti-bullying campaign if it is to succeed.

The research on school climate suggests that the principal is the single most important person to have involved in the program. Researchers have consistently reported that the principal's leadership and vision predict the degree to which the staff is able to effect needed reform, particularly in disciplinary matters (Walker, Colvin, & Ramsey, 1995).

With a committee to evaluate problems, set goals, and plan programming, the potential problem of resistance is at least minimized, if not eliminated. Input from teachers and parents is particularly essential if the program is to be taken seriously by those who will be most involved. The cultivation of student leaders is very important because it is these individuals who can promote the program to other students and lead by example as more adaptive interpersonal relationships are encouraged in the building. Student members can preview materials and predict how other students will react to them and can report quickly if the program is not going well. Including students also communicates an egalitarian and democratic stance, which is an important feature of this effort.

In addition to involving all groups represented within an institution, planning may involve outside agencies. For example, mental health and social service agencies may participate in planning if troubled students are identified and referred for intensive services.

Taking a Stand against Bullying

The basic characteristics of an anti-bullying school are grounded in a global affirmation: students do not bully one another. As stated on a button distributed to Norwegian schoolchildren: "Friends do not bully friends."

The first task for the program is to set standards and consequences for bullying. Much information is available regarding effective procedures for setting reasonable rules and regulations in school and classrooms (e.g., Walker, Colvin, & Ramsey, 1995). The most important principle in setting rules is that all groups should have input.

Evaluation and Setting Goals

Since each school or facility where an anti-bullying campaign will be initiated is different—with different constituencies and differing constellations of problems—it is essential that information be collected that will allow targeting the program to specific needs. In addition, funding agencies, parents, students, and school boards need to be informed regarding possible outcomes of the anti-bullying project. Chapter Four includes a detailed plan for evaluating a school or facility for this purpose.

Outcome goals set the direction of the anti-bullying campaign and facilitate communication to students and other groups about what actions are going to be taken. Goals should be set by the committee and approved by the appropriate legal bodies. We recommend that program goals be submitted to the student council for approval, even if this body has no legal standing.

Goals should be stated clearly and, where it does no violence to aims, expressed in measurable forms. It is generally helpful to list "markers," or indicators associated with each goal, to facilitate evaluation. An example is shown below:

Goal: A significant reduction in the monthly rate of bullying will be achieved by May 15.

Markers: 1. A reduction of at least 25% between pre and post-evaluation periods will be noted in the percentage of students who select choices 2, 3, or 4 on Form B, item B-3.

          2. A majority of students interviewed in May will agree that less bullying occurs than did previously.

3. A drop of at least 20% will be noted in incident reports of fights or other aggressive behavior (averaged over April and May vs. September and October).

The process of agreeing on these goals will also help to hone the quality of the program.

Major goals, broadly stated, can be identified prior to the evaluation. This would be reasonable because there will be strong agreement on selected aims. However, the establishment of the majority of specific goals should wait for completion of the evaluation. This will allow a clearer picture of the school or program to emerge, which in turn will expedite development of utilitarian goals.

Before the evaluation is designed and conducted, and before the setting of anti-bullying goals, a useful starting point might be to establish a student Bill of Rights. This will require a great deal of thought and debate before a final statement is written. The statement of rights is an excellent precursor to setting limits on behavior. Of course, these statements will be different for every school, but the following is provided as a rough example:

Each student at _____ Middle School has the right to

1. learn in a safe and friendly place.

2. grow and learn without encountering harassment about race, gender, religion, or ethnic group.

3. be free of harassment about appearance, dress, learning style, interests, or behaviors.

4. receive the help of caring adults if any of the above rights are violated.

Disseminating Information

Public Meeting

An excellent start for the anti-bullying campaign is to carefully plan and hold a large, public kickoff meeting, perhaps away from school grounds. If space pressures do not allow parents, staff members, and students to assemble, separate meetings may be held for each group. These gatherings should be coordinated carefully so that all groups understand the basics of the proposed program. The setting should be as pleasant as possible, perhaps with refreshments provided.

One idea would be to kick off the anti-bullying campaign with a "No More Bullying Day." Speakers could be brought in, and members of the planning committee could present facts and figures about bullying. Many useful materials and resources are listed in the appendices (pp. 145–148). One of our favorites is the videotape *Set Straight on Bullies,* which can be purchased from the National School Safety Center. The video is an excellent ice breaker and discussion starter.

Conceptual material presented at initial meetings will vary, based on the specifics of the program in question and results of the evaluation study. Ample time should be allotted for questions and discussions. However, we have found that teachers and students react well to the following list and order of topics.

    I.   Definition of Bullying

   II.   Bullying Behaviors

        A. Teasing

        B. Verbal harassment

        C. Unwanted touches

        D. Physical attacks: hits, kicks, scratches, pokes, etc.

        E. Ostracism

  III.   Numbers of Young People Hurt by Bullying

        A. Incidence and prevalence figures

        B. Negative outcomes

             1. For victims

             2. For bullies

  IV.   Description of the Anti-Bullying Project

        A. New (or old) conduct rules and consequences

        B. Schedule of schoolwide assemblies and their topics

        C. Classroom activities

Printed Resources

Olweus stressed the importance of information. Thus, one feature of the initial meeting or kickoff day would be to present information about the breadth of the problem. Information from Chapters One and Two of this book could serve as the primary resource. In addition, a pamphlet on bullying is available from the William Gladden Foundation (Hoover, in press; see page 146). The National School Safety Center is also a primary resource for materials.

Printed materials should be prepared specifically for each group in the institution. For example, targeted audiences in a school would be students, parents, teachers, and staff. Enough materials should be prepared for several mailings. A newsletter relating progress on anti-bullying goals could also be sent out.

Other Ideas for Information Dissemination

Buttons. Norwegian school personnel arranged to have buttons designed and distributed to students and their parents with the simple message, "Friends do not bully friends." Students were encouraged to wear these buttons to school as a reminder of the anti-bullying ethos of the school. This procedure may work well in some American schools, and button makers are readily available. Excellent templates for buttons are provided in *Bully Proofing* (Garrity et al. 1995; see resources list, p. 146).

Posters. Anti-bullying and anti-violence posters are available from several sources listed on pp. 145–148. In addition, posters can be developed by members of the committee; perhaps a parent who is a specialist in graphic design can be located. A very beneficial activity would be to incorporate the bullying reduction program into art classes and have students design the posters. Posters should be changed periodically in order to retain their communication value.

Electronic and Print Media. Get the anti-bullying message out via public and commercial television stations. Newspapers and radio are other media that can be used to communicate the message. Many localities now have local call-in shows; these programs might make an excellent forum for public discussions of bullying. A representative of the planning committee should write a piece for each issue of the institution's newsletter and for such groups as the PTA. If these outlets do not exist, perhaps the anti-bullying campaign group could start one.

Mailings. A central feature of the Norwegian bully prevention and reduction project was mailings to all Norwegian householders (Olweus, 1991). A letter should be sent to parents informing them about the project and inviting them to attend information and planning meetings. At various times during the year, letters should be sent to remind parents about the program and to ask them to talk about it with their children.

A brochure should be developed that contains the information outlined above along with a list of contact names, addresses, and phone numbers. The most important information to disseminate in this way is details of the code of conduct. Parents are asked to discuss these with their offspring.

The large-scale meetings are meant to kick off the program and to get essential information about bullying into the hands of students, parents, and teachers. However, the real work will be completed in classrooms. Here, in more intimate groupings, teachers and counselors can follow up with class discussions, role plays, and art projects. Every effort should be made to incorporate these activities into the curriculum, perhaps during periodic "Down with Bullying Weeks." Suggestions for activities to facilitate these practices are provided in the final section.

Classroom Activities

It is easier to incorporate bullying materials and prevention activities into the middle school curriculum when the school has integrated programming and its teams of teachers meet regularly for planning purposes. If the school operates more traditionally, then social studies, English, or health teachers may be most interested in these resources. In some schools, counselors meet regularly with students, and they would provide a reasonable venue for these activities.

The same information presented in large groups should be readministered periodically in classrooms. In addition, videotapes and other media can be used in the classroom. Encourage students to bring in examples of bullying episodes they discover in the newspaper and from the popular media. While discussion and role playing are important features of the program, it is important to keep reminding students about bullying facts—the damage it can do, what it is, and the harmful myth that it is normal behavior. In addition, the bill of student rights and disciplinary policies regarding harassment should be known well by every student.

In the paragraphs below, ideas are provided for initiating discussions in classrooms. Note that these are a limited set; the sky is the limit in terms of what can be done about sensitizing adolescents to bullying problems. Remember that, as with any controversial topic, an atmosphere open to many shades of opinion is absolutely required if discussions are to be pedagogically useful. For students this age, good practices also include the use of an advance organizer or topic starter, such as a video or a short reading assignment. In addition, it is important to summarize the information, bring it to some type of closure, and then hold students responsible for it in some way.

In our discussions with young people, no topic roused more heated debate than did teasing. As noted in Chapter Two, students recognize that verbal interplay in the style of teasing is a very complex matter. Put most simply, it can be inclusive, humorous, friendly behavior or it can represent damaging, hateful, ugly harassment. Many factors are involved in predicting how a young person will receive a "joshing" remark.

A series of discussion questions is provided (p. 151). We developed this list based on issues raised in discussions with secondary students, but most of the concepts should be accessible to students as young as the fifth grade. A list of teasing facts, do's, and don'ts is included on page 153. This list could be used instead of more open-ended discussions with younger students or as a conversation starter for any age group.

Role plays are also very useful. Several bullying and interpersonal dispute scenarios have been prepared for instructional use, based on our conversations with teachers and students in middle schools (pp. 123–127). Considerable groundwork must be laid before role plays will be successful. Trust between students and educators must be in evidence before role plays will be effective. Another variable is the willingness of students to "let go," that is, to lose themselves in the emotions of the scene. Students will be more willing to act out parts and then discuss them if teachers also show themselves willing to do so! The drama teacher is an important resource in this regard.

Another excellent lead-in or follow-up activity to teasing discussions is to observe television situation comedies for put downs. Together, the moderator and students develop criteria for what constitutes a put down or an instance of cruel humor. These criteria are developed into a checklist or tally sheet. Students then watch the shows and rate them for verbal aggression. Most students will gain a new insight into the potential for misunderstanding and damage that this type of humor entails. Rousing discussions of First Amendment rights, debates about the effects of teasing, and moral questions about the rightness or wrongness of actions have resulted from these conversations. Even racial and ethnic differences in humor can be broached because of certain popular shows.

A Minnesota teacher related her experience with a method for the intellectual criticism of media. Students watched the show "Roseanne" and deconstructed the humor in the show. The discussion that ensued was one of the most vibrant and worthwhile media critiques we have ever heard about: students concluded that the intended theme of the show was that, despite their rough edges and sharp-edged humor, Dan and Roseanne loved their children deeply. However, the tone of the humor was so angry and cruel that the students felt that in reality the children would be damaged. The difficulty is that the show really is funny, with the result that the anger becomes too beguiling. Darlene, Becky, and DJ, it was concluded, would suffer from low self-esteem if they existed outside the glass box. Creative activities such as this can get many bullying issues onto the table in a manner students find quite palatable. No substitute in teaching has ever been found for creativity!

Addressing Student Attitudes

Chapter Two reviewed a study of student attitudes leading either to bullying or to failure on the part of bystanders to intervene (Oliver, Hoover, & Hazler, 1994). Two of them are considered below as possible dialogue and study topics.

Victims brought it on themselves. Students can be led, through a discussion of this attitude, to the important sociological principle of blaming the victim. This is one area where conversations about a topic readily accessible to most individuals, namely their own oppression by bullies, can segue into the broader areas of gender and race relations.

Bullying helps students by making them tougher. We discussed this with a group of students in a small South Dakota town, and they came up with the fascinating insight that punishing someone for inappropriate behavior or for actions considered undesirable by "the group" was neither a healthy nor useful way to change behavior. This could have great implications for their future as parents. In addition, the discussion came around to the notion of individuality and the related idea that perhaps the group is not always right, a wonderful topic for a classroom in a democratic society.

Summary

- A committee representing parents, staff members, and students (where age is appropriate) must be set up to plan the schoolwide anti-bullying campaign.

- Participation of the principal is a central feature in the success or failure of schoolwide discipline programs and thus also in a bullying prevention program.

- Evaluation is an essential feature of a bullying reduction program (see Chapter Four).

- A firm stance opposed to bullying—backed up by a discipline plan—is an essential component of an anti-bullying campaign.

- Establishing goals and indicators of meeting these goals will improve the program. Goals should be stated clearly and in such a way that the level of achievement can be agreed upon.

- Developing a student Bill of Rights makes an effective lead-in to development of goals and setting behavioral expectations.

- A kickoff public meeting, or several such meetings, is important. This gathering should be informational in nature. In fact, the dissemination of bullying information was considered central to the success of the Norwegian Ministry of Education program.

- Printed resources must be developed and distributed. Information should be made available to parents periodically. All available media should be used.

- Buttons, posters, and mailings could be used to maintain public and student interest and awareness.

- Teasing is a confusing topic for students this age and is often seen as bullying. Because of these issues, it is an especially important topic around which to center classroom discussions and activities.

- Role plays are an important tool in developing an understanding of bullying.

- Media criticism has helped students gain insight into the possible role of humor in harassment and bullying.

- Two student attitudes about bullying discovered through research deserve attention from teachers: bullying is the fault of victims, and bullying helps students by teaching them what is acceptable to the group.

CHAPTER 6

FAMILY ISSUES IN BULLYING

Perhaps it is not surprising to find that the families of bullies seldom receive our sympathetic attention. However, family relationships are often central to defining each of us as individuals. Thus the relationships of bullying and victimized youth to their families might be central in understanding these issues.

Clearly, many factors interact to spawn violent actions. However, violence is largely learned behavior; and the primary source of most early learning is the family home. Behavior that does not make sense in the context of the school may make sense in the context of home and family.

Family issues are not tackled in an attempt to blame families. Rather, the purpose of this chapter is to piece together what is known about families of both habitually bullying students and those who chronically experience victimization in order to understand family patterns that contribute to aggression and victimization. The dynamics of bully and scapegoat families should provide clues for treatment procedures in situations where problems are transported from home to school. Family dynamics that may lead to bullying behavior are examined first. In a later section, we probe the family lives of scapegoats.

Bullies and Their Families

The families of bullies are in many ways disconnected, and their members dwell in an emotionally cold environment. Yet there are occasional contrasting periods of overheated emotion and anger. In some sense, bullying families are also victim families.

Olweus (1980; 1984) identified four factors in the home environment that were positively related to the development of aggressive behavior: (1) negativism, in particular, by the mother of the child; (2) indifference, neglect, and rejection by primary caregivers; (3) permissiveness for aggressive acts; and (4) harsh, punitive child-rearing methods. These factors were found when children who were identified as bullies were asked about the nature of their home life and their relationships with parents.

Bullies were more likely than others to report that their parents did not like them very much or did not spend much time talking with them. They were also much more likely to endure violent modes of punishment. In this connection, bullies also noted more negativity toward and less identification with their fathers.

British researchers found similar familial patterns. English bullies were up to ten times more likely than were other children to report that their family had problems at home (Stephenson & Smith, 1989). Inconsistent disciplinary practices were noted, but these were embedded in a context of conflicted relationships, characterized by frequent marital discord along with financial and social difficulties.

A clear picture of the family life of many bullies emerges when the above observations are paired with the work of American researchers, such as Eron and Patterson. For example, Eron (1987) concluded that the best predictors of future aggression at age eight were: (1) rejection by one or both parents, (2) extensive use of physical punishment, (3) lack of nurturing, and (4) parental disharmony.

Eron established that adults who had been childhood bullies tended to have children who were bullies. Further, as adults, these former childhood bullies were more likely to have been convicted of violent crimes, more likely to be abusive with their spouses, and more likely to be severely punitive with their children. These long-term consequences are largely echoed in longitudinal data from the Scandinavian countries.

In summarizing familial factors in bullying, Olweus (1980) noted that the following six factors consistently emerged:

1. Home lives were characterized by emotional frigidity.

2. There existed greater likelihood of chaotic home organization.

3. The families of bullies tended to be socially isolated.

4. Frequent parental conflict and disharmony was noted.

5. Child-rearing practices were largely ineffective.

6. Rigidity in maintaining family order was often observed.

Educators must consider the possibility that some bullies come to school from such families. While prohibitions against aggressive and insulting behavior may help the situation in the short term, many bullies may be best helped by referrals for family counseling. What, if anything, characterizes the familial patterns of students who are frequently harassed?

Victims and Their Families: The Cramped Hothouse

Important facets of parent-child and family relations among victim families are only sketchily developed at this point. Surprisingly, what is known suggests that similarities exist between the family environments of bullies and some victims (Olweus, 1978; Chazan, 1989). Parallels may be seen in the similar lack of consistent disciplinary practices, in the existence of child-parent relationship difficulties, the frequent presence of marital problems, manifestations of family financial problems, and relationships outside the home.

However, one predominant difference between families of bullies and chronic victims is noted: victim families appear overly emotionally involved and entangled. Many families of victims may become deeply involved in responding to the child's oppression. Teachers and counselors must be sensitive to the possibility that relational problems in the homes of scapegoats are an effect of victimization rather than its cause.

Olweus (1978) characterized chronic victims as "whipping boys" who were sensitive and passive in nature, close to parents, and typically reared in aggression-inhibiting and not very masculine environments. That is, they have seemingly missed out on, or not adjusted to, the "rough and tumble" side of childhood. It is noteworthy that Olweus originally studied only male bullying and victimization. Other researchers characterize the nature of the parents' involvement as overprotective and over-consuming in terms of the time spent together (Munthe, 1989). This over-dependence on parental support may leave the school-age child socially ineffective, insecure, and disadvantaged around peers. Many such youngsters deal much better with the predictability of adults than with the more chaotic child culture.

It is unclear whether closer relations with parents precedes, follows, or both precedes and follows victim status. The degree of the child's need for the closeness, security, and emotional comfort supplied by the home increases in direct proportion to suffering experienced at the hands of peers. Again, this is speculation; but it is based on longitudinal data that clearly identify long-term consequences of chronic victimization, such as increased anxiety, depression, and troubled heterosexual relationship formation (Gilmartin, 1987; Olweus, 1992; Robins, 1966).

Given that status as either a bully or a chronic victim implies that predictable family difficulties may be present, it remains to discuss possible solutions. In the next sections of the chapter, potential solutions are developed.

Counseling with Families of Bullies

A good starting point is to acknowledge that bullying at school should, at least, be considered a warning sign of family problems. Thus appropriate screening for this possibility is indicated. To aid in this screening process, we suggest the use of a brief eight-point checklist.

Brief Screening

The elements of the checklist, found on page 157, deal primarily with the issues of family structure, problem-solving abilities, expectations, history, and risk of negative outcomes. While such a brief measure has obvious limitations, the questions reflect the relevant dimensions of familial functioning and are based on the best available research. When combined with other pertinent information available to the professional, it will aid the decision-making process and help answer the question, "Can I work productively with this family pursuant to their difficulties with bullying or victimization?"

In the process of arriving at a decision for each question, cultural differences and considerations must be weighed. For example, in many Latino families, the role of the parent is traditionally one of such strong authority that minimal input from children would be sought or accepted in family decision processes (Samovar & Porter, 1991).

If two or more responses are answered in the negative, then referral to outside agencies for family support and counseling is indicated. The only exception to this rule of thumb would be question eight, concerned with physical or sexual abuse. All states now have mandatory child-abuse reporting laws for helping professionals; the reasonable suspicion of abuse or neglect requires referral to appropriate authorities and may short-circuit the potential for the development of a counseling relationship with the family.

Directions for Counseling Intervention

Two primary directions for the process of counseling are implied, should the counselor decide to work with a family. The initial goal would be to *increase the emotional closeness and togetherness of the family.* A second direction is to *help family members achieve greater structure and consistency.*

Increasing Closeness in Family Relationships

In the process of defining and developing the relationship between the counselor and family, the modeling of open, direct, caring communication will support the goal of increasing the family's emotional closeness. The counseling relationship should be used as a tool for teaching effective communication, for demonstrating comfort with emotional closeness, and for modeling respectful behaviors. The respect and dignity accorded the family by the counselor not only shows how closeness begins, but it often communicates the unspoken message that respecting others facilitates group functioning.

The information that counseling is likely to improve family members' quality of life should be clearly enunciated during initial sessions. This conclusion is supported by solid research in the field (Gurman & Kniskern, 1991).

One of the important lessons learned from studies of human development is that taking the perspective of the other person is necessary for future intimacy. Therefore, efforts by the counselor to fully hear out each participant's concerns will advance the counseling process and provide an experience of closeness in communication and a lesson on how to bond with others. In short, working with the families of aggressive children requires considerable empathy.

Looking for Agreements, Similarities, and Harmonies. The early stages of developing the relationship with the family will likely involve a discussion of how each member currently views the family, as well as how they envision the future of the family. In facilitating this discussion, the counselor may further relational intimacy by highlighting agreements. Agreements may be found in similarities of taste, features of appearance, interests, hobbies, and the like.

Family Sculpture. There are benefits that may accrue to both the counselor and family by clarifying the extent of the emotional closeness/distance in the relationships in the early stage of counseling. For the counselor, as well as the family, knowing how close family members perceive that they are to one another is helpful in setting baselines and assessing progress.

Family sculpting, developed by David Kantor (see Piercy & Sprenkle, 1986, p. 57), is a technique by which symbolic processes and events are portrayed in the dimension of space, and analogies are drawn from this. Members are asked to describe their family through the physical placement of one another in frozen postures, that is, to make a sculpture of family members frozen in time and space. A variation on this theme is the use of tokens or models to achieve the same ends.

Each family member is given a turn at sculpting their relationships to all other family members. The best comments to be made are simple statements of fact about the arrangement, delivered in a nonjudgmental tone. It might be discovered, for example, that one member of the family is able to secure the attention of other members given the distance and posturing pictured.

If participants are strongly motivated, and the counselor is sufficiently comfortable in dealing with potent emotions, the use of the family sculpting technique may release unexpressed emotions in even the most distanced families. A counselor who can comfortably and safely guide family members through safe expressions of pain will likely facilitate increased bonding.

The voicing of stored anger and resentment, when done in a physically safe environment, allows the family to get past some possibly exaggerated fears and blocks in communication and often provides opportunity for teachable moments. Anger is often a double-edged sword; while it presents a threat to relationships, it also offers an opportunity to explore new ways of interrelating.

Other uses of family sculpting include work with over-involved families, such as the families of chronically victimized children. In such cases, sculpting is used to disengage the clients from emotional experience and thus facilitate insight into past and present situations in the family (Piercy & Sprenkle, 1986). The technique may be modified to allow for the enactment of particularly problematic occasions in the daily life of the family. Such mundane scenes as doing chores or eating meals may be spatially pictured as a stimulus to problem solving.

Relabeling and Reframing Techniques. Group cohesion can be enhanced by helping family members reframe bullying as a problem belonging to the group rather than to one member. This may be done by identifying behaviors that maintain aggression, for example, a wink from one of the parents after first expressing dismay over a child's fighting with a neighbor.

In reframing, the helping professional describes the target behavior in an understandable, realistic context. In doing this, it is important to take into account the family's current belief system when looking at an altered context. Redefinitions must be believable if family members are to embrace and use them in changing their circumstances. The counselor may start by asking, "In what way is the behavior at issue either helpful or protective in relation to others, and other family members in particular?"

For example, the distance and lack of supervision by parents might be reframed as an expression of the trust that the parents have in their offspring. This level of confidence may then be characterized as requiring reevaluation, given the problems the youngster is experiencing at school. Alternatively, exaggerated trust might be reframed as the excessive giving of "space," that is, exaggerated respect for the individuality of family members. From this slightly altered perspective, counselors may find parents more receptive to addressing the problem.

Hunting for Strengths and Affirming Feelings. Because many bullies and their families experience anger and distress in their home relationships, their focus may be on problems and deficits. Two therapeutic directions may help families leave this deficit model behind. First, individuals must be convinced that it is safe to feel and express feelings. Second, the strengths, assets, and "buried treasures" within each member of the family, as well as the family as a whole, must be emphasized. Barriers to feeling are likely to be encountered; emotional distance requires that many emotions be avoided. Thus it is therapeutic to affirm feelings and to provide opportunities for them to be safely expressed. In this connection, family members should be given the assignment of setting aside a brief, special time each week for emotional sharing.

Developing family stories is another method of supporting a positive, strength-based direction. Each family member is asked to recall a pleasant memory from the past, as well as an occasion when the problem of bullying was absent or was handled well. This not only provides an opportunity for positive, shared experiences, but also assumes the absence of the problem. The question may be posed as directly as, "Tell me about occasions when the problem is not a problem."

Other Techniques. At least five other techniques may aid the process of increasing family cohesion. These are listed below. Descriptions of these specific methods are beyond the scope of this book. The interested reader, however, is directed to excellent introductory family counseling texts (see Fenell & Weinhold, 1989; Nichols & Schwartz, 1991).

1. Reverse Role Playing (RRP)

2. Communication Skills Training

3. Highlighting Common Ground

4. Making Toys Together

5. Family Time

All of these methods provide counselors the opportunity to "tighten" relationships in the family. A second direction for intervention with bullies is to help parents establish more structure in the unit's day-to-day life.

Improving Structure

Several opportunities are likely to arise during the counseling sessions for improving the family's structure. For example, frequent opportunities for establishing clear and consistent limits typically present themselves during sessions. The process of settling administrative details, such as providing informed consent and acknowledging the limits of confidentiality, are in themselves structuring acts and may be used as a model for setting limits. The logical consequences of breaking established rules should be spelled out at the time of their development, in order to show family members how this can be done gently and dispassionately. Consequences should be appropriate to the developmental age of the child, as well as in keeping with the importance to the family of the particular rule. Physically punitive consequences should be carefully avoided in favor of restrictions and loss of privileges.

Parents may be given the assignment of agreeing to and writing down family rules. Success by the family with setting rules will tell the counselor a lot about what might be expected in working with the family. That is, if the couple is unable to accomplish this task, and if negotiation and problem-solving skills are not present nor readily learned, then positive outcomes are unlikely and referral for marital counseling is indicated.

Otherwise, counseling may focus on the teaching of alternative parenting strategies that emphasize consistency in parent-child relations. Behavioral management techniques, such as those described in detail by Patterson (1982), are likely to be most effective with those families where executive decision making is practiced, that is, those families with an authoritarian style of parenting.

For parents of adolescents, some resistance to reducing control is likely to be encountered. Proposed changes should be framed as a recognition of the increasing age, growth, and maturity evidenced by the adolescent. As a result, caregivers may learn to "catch themselves," or recognize the early signs of overheated relationships, such as increased breathing and heart rate and tenseness in muscles and jaw. In particular, adolescents may be taught methods of taking a "time out," simple deep breathing and relaxation, or how to reschedule the conflict to a less emotional time. In other words, they would be learning to manage the possible aggression and to frame the overall process as positively as possible to help minimize possible resistance.

Counseling Families of Victims

The families of bullies and victims, as noted above, share some features. Because of this, many of the interventions and strategies discussed in connection with bullies may also be applied to victim families.

A primary distinguishing pattern of these families is the possibility of parental over-involvement. As a consequence, the principle direction that counseling is likely to assume with the family of a victim is toward greater emotional separation of family members. A secondary goal is to encourage greater involvement outside the home, particularly with peers. Parents, and even siblings, may be enlisted in supporting this second goal, as both their permission and encouragement of peer relations may make a crucial difference.

Anticipating Defensiveness

The first issue to consider is the likely entrenched defensive posture that the family will assume. After all, a parent naturally tends to protect a victimized child. The counselor would do well to support this family strength and to verbally applaud the family for caring so much. It also might be recognized by the counselor early on that, in fact, behavioral science really does not know which comes first, parental over-involvement or the child's victimization.

Support of Grieving

Another valid direction for the counselor to take involves finding a way to recognize and validate the hurt and to support the grieving process that the family is likely undergoing. Any number of possible therapeutic interventions for children and adolescents, as well as adults, is detailed in Alicia Cook and Daniel Dworkin's book, *Helping the Bereaved* (1992).

The counselor should first assess family members' knowledge of the grief process and their relative acceptance or rejection of the associated emotions. If little is known, then appropriate bibliotherapeutic reading materials and referrals may be initiated (see Chapter

Nine). Or the counselor may wish to inform the family of the likelihood that they are experiencing the emotions of shock, denial, bargaining, depression, or anger, and to help them take the path to eventual acceptance.

Fostering Autonomy

The primary direction that counseling is likely to take with the families of chronic scapegoats is toward decreasing the level of parental intensity and increasing clarification of members' unique identities. To better discern the possible degree of emotional cohesion and enmeshment present in the family, and to provide a measurement of gains made in counseling toward greater individuation, three brief assessment methods may be used. First, family sculpture may be used. Second, drawing and using an "ecomap" with the family is often beneficial. Finally, the counselor could use a brief, descriptive checklist of family behaviors associated with emotional over-involvement.

Ecomaps

Ecomaps may prove helpful not only for assessment purposes, for graphically illustrating the level of social isolation and support available to the family, but also for purposes of taking the blame and focus of family members off the individual and moving it toward the environment. Ecomaps may be repeated during counseling as a measure of progress attained (Hartman & Laird, 1983).

In creating an ecomap, the counselor looks at the total environment of the family and asks individual members to characterize the nature of their connections with aspects of the environment. Ecomaps are typically drawn by first noting the names of each family member of the household inside a large circle. Outside of the circle, smaller circles are then drawn and labeled as friends, bullies, antagonists, extended family members, church, work and sources of family income, memberships in social and charitable organizations, recreation, the family home, and any other ecological or environmental factors significantly affecting the family's life.

An example of an ecomap for an over-enmeshed family is shown in Figure 6.1.

Figure 6.1: Ecomap for an Over-Enmeshed Family

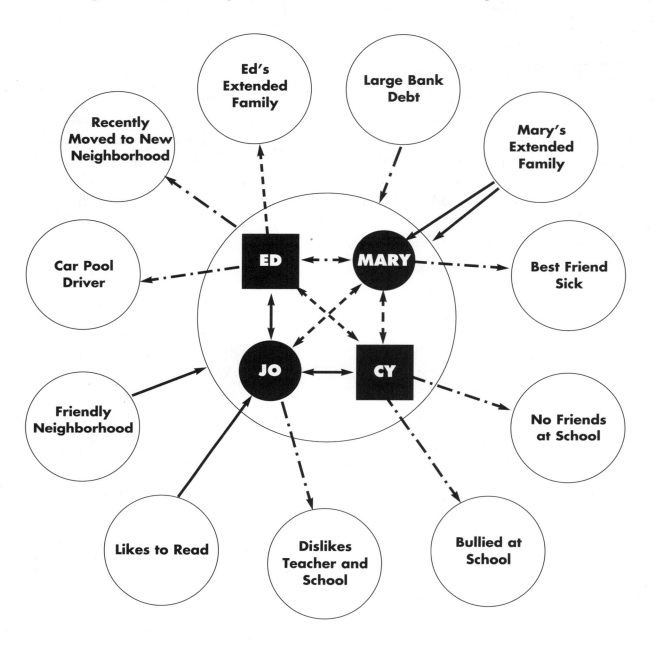

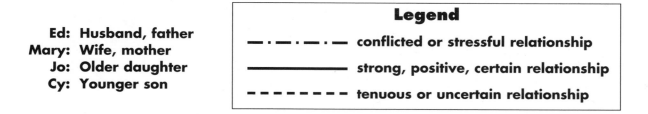

Ed: Husband, father
Mary: Wife, mother
Jo: Older daughter
Cy: Younger son

Legend

— · — · — conflicted or stressful relationship

————— strong, positive, certain relationship

– – – – tenuous or uncertain relationship

The picture that will typically emerge from the completed ecomap is one in which relations inside the family are characterized as strong, but relations to the environment are generally few in number and costly in terms of energy loss.

Enmeshment Checklist

The enmeshment checklist provided in the appendix on p. 131 is a simple attempt to denote the major characteristics of enmeshed, overly involved families (see Becvar & Becvar, 1988; and Fenell & Weinhold, 1989). Each item may be marked as "yes" or "no" by the counselor as it is reviewed with the family or it may simply be given to the family to complete together as a homework assignment.

In using the checklist, the counselor should provide assurance that concern is a very helpful and protective way for families to interact. Further, at some point, most people will experience too much or too little closeness—overdoing is, after all, a most human trait.

Working with Family Beliefs

The counselor begins this process by starting with the parents and asking each member to voice his or her beliefs about family togetherness and what the family should do when one of its members is harassed. The counselor may wish to employ a flip chart to record responses so that the information is readily available and summarized accurately.

After the parents have stated their beliefs about how the family should come to the aid of a victimized member, the involved individual is asked to respond. The counselor may support the victimized child if the child voices the appropriate desire to gain greater independence in dealing with the problem. The counselor's role in this process is to support the rights of each individual in the family to extra-familial identities, interests, privacy, pursuits, and friends.

If the family beliefs are found to be unreasonable and intrusive in dealing with the victimized child, then looking at consequences, active questioning, sharing of developmental information, or even disputation on logical or developmental grounds may be required from the counselor.

In this regard, cognitive approaches that have shown much promise in application to the individual may be adapted for use with the family (see Corey, 1991, pp. 324–368).

It must be emphasized that for counseling interventions to be most effective, a combination of strategies should address all aspects of the issue, including the cognitive, behavioral, and emotional realms.

Summary

- Family and counseling strategies for both bully and victim families were described as part of a holistic approach. They were recommended for inclusion in a comprehensive response that also addresses school and community environmental values and issues.

- The families of many bullies are characterized by a cold emotional environment, punctuated with frequent bouts of anger.

- The parents of bullies often exercise little restraint on aggression; home life may be confused and disjointed.

- Olweus observed that families of many chronic victims are characterized by over-involvement. It was pointed out that this may result from, rather than cause, victimization.

- A brief method for the preliminary screening of families for referral to community resources was noted and suggestions offered.

- Family assessment issues were detailed for families of both bullies and victims, including the use of family sculpting models.

- Brief school or program-based family counseling interventions and activities for work with families of both bullies and victims were described.

- Fostering greater family integration and identity is the guiding principle for counseling with families of bullies.

- The use of the counseling relationship to model behaviors, illustrate empathy, clarify communication, and highlight change was also explained in relation to work with families of bullies.

- Relabeling and reframing strategies were discussed as methods for alerting families to strengths that could provide direction for improvement.

- Support for greater autonomy among family members was found to be a principal direction for counseling with the families of victimized children.

- Methods of counseling with families of victimized children included support of the grieving process, the use of ecomaps, and examination of familial beliefs.

CHAPTER 7

PIKAS'S COMMON CONCERN METHOD

A helpful framework for intervention in bullying problems is the Common Concern Method (CCM) developed by Pikas (1989b). The CCM is the only counseling model targeted specifically at bullying problems; Pikas also intended that both bullies and scapegoats learn new interactional skills through the process.

The CCM framework is a useful tool for classroom teachers, counselors, social workers, and human-relations professionals who possess good interpersonal skills. The CCM method develops clear directions for the interviewing process. However, effective intervention requires more than just knowledge of counseling tactics. Truly effective intervention calls for all the human relations skills, finesse, wisdom, and know-how at practitioners' disposal. With this in mind, several cautions are offered.

Potential Problems with the CCM Approach

Individuals practicing the CCM approach should first spend several hours in reflection on the process. This also requires a thorough self-examination. Given the strong emotions engendered by peer abuse, this reflection should include a review of one's knowledge and the level of awareness of one's emotional triggers and limits. In this regard, we agree with

Long's assertion (1995) that counselors' effectiveness will be limited by the extent to which their emotional reactions feed conflictual flames.

As the practitioner considers his or her needs prior to initiating CCM sessions, reflection on control needs is strongly suggested. We are all sometimes blind to our own desire to manage situations. The ability to share power is central to effective use of CCM. Participants must be empowered; according to Pikas, troubled students often must be treated as equals to the adult participant if a successful resolution of the crisis is to be achieved. Persons with high control needs will probably feel threatened by this form of intervention.

The CCM approach should be part of a larger anti-bullying system that enjoys the support of administrators and colleagues. The CCM effort is probably doomed to discouraging failure if it lacks systemic support.

A final peril to avoid is either-or, black-white thinking followed by a one-size-fits-all response to bullying behaviors. We have a cultural tendency to look for quick fixes and over-simplified answers. When that is combined with fatigue from dealing with too much frustration and stress and with the increasingly popular hard-nosed attitude toward aggressive youth, there is a likelihood for failure. It is very difficult to remain objective in the face of aggressive behavior, but in the CCM it is a must.

Clear limitations to CCM exist in some bullying situations. In particular, difficulty may be experienced in cases where concern about the victim is absent, cooperation is missing, and all relations with adults and authority figures are negative. These are symptoms of relationship starvation, and the place to start working with these children is to help them develop at least one positive, satisfying relationship with a caring adult. In these cases, practitioners would look to youth and family service agencies, complemented by community mentoring resources. With most other limiting situations, the effectiveness of CCM will vary according to bullies' level of maturity and ability to form attachments.

With the above concerns in mind, the counselor will be ready to undertake CCM sessions. The CCM and recommended alterations are described in the following paragraphs.

Common Concern Procedures

The primary thrust of CCM is to build empathy among bullies for their victims. To accomplish this goal, students take ownership of the problem and responsibility for its resolution. The bullies reach a "common concern" for the fate of the victim. Once this vital point is reached, the students can explore new ways of relating more successfully, facilitated as needed by the counselor. The Suggestive Command Method (SCM) is frequently used in conjunction with CCM when the victim's behavior has been "provocative," that is, where it is clear that actions on the part of the weaker student initiated a bullying episode. It differs mainly by placing the interventionist in a more directive and authoritative role with the student.

The structures of both CCM and SCM are straightforward. The underlying rationale is equally direct: understanding and appealing to the plight of victims leads to reductions or outright cessation of the bullying. Some experts find this straightforwardness of CCM distressing and too simple (Olweus, 1992, personal communication). Nonetheless, we view the potential benefits of CCM as outweighing the problems. For instance, the goal of fostering empathy is well supported by research that demonstrates that aggression diminishes in the face of increased empathy.

The Initial Bully Interview

The individual CCM sessions combine both investigation and intervention components. Pikas recommends that the first interview be based on information obtained from adult observers. This protects the victim from being accused by the bully of having "told on" him. For the same reason, it is also suggested that the bully(ies) be interviewed first. If several students harassed an individual victim, then interviews should be carried out in successive sessions, with about 15 to 20 minutes allowed for each conference. The first dialogue is summarized in the five principal points enumerated below, along with suggested remarks.

1. Opening:

   "I would like to talk to you because I've heard you have been mean to Paul."

2. Invitation to disclose, relate, and act:

   "What do you know about it?"

3. Transition:

   "All right, we've talked about it long enough."

4. Resolution and taking responsibility:

   "What should be done? What do you suggest?"

5. The closing:

   "That's good. We'll meet again in a week; then you can tell me how you've been getting on."

The degree of emotional contact recommended by Pikas for each of the "marker points" listed above is represented by the plot shown in Figure 7.1. The level of contact is to build during most of the interview, in a sense laying the groundwork for taking problem-solving responsibility, which is best accomplished in a climate of reduced arousal.

The entire focus of the first session is for the bully to understand and believe that the victim's situation is something to be concerned about. There are a number of practical methods available to counselors for enhancing empathy and developing rapport with the bully. These rapport-building skills are beyond the scope of this book. The interested reader is referred to Ivey's (1988) microskills model for a more in-depth exploration of this topic.

FIGURE 7.1: THE CURVE OF EMOTIONAL CONTACT ACCORDING TO THE COMMON CONCERN METHOD (CCM)

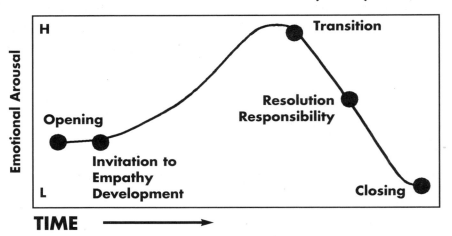

Strong experiences of common concern about tormenting the victim

Communication on equal terms between the counselor and the student suspected of bullying

- "I would like to talk to you because I've heard you have been mean to Paul."

- "What do you know about it?"

- "All right, we've talked about it long enough."

- "What to do? What do you suggest?"

- "That's good. We'll meet again in a week; then you can tell me how you've been getting on."

Points #1 & #2—Opening and Supporting Empathy Development. The opening remarks are simply a statement of the purpose of the interview—"I would like to talk to you because I've heard you have been mean to Paul,"—followed closely by a very broad, open-ended question—"What do you know about it?" As was noted by Pikas (1989b), the most important phase of the interview is between the second and third points. Because arriving at a shared concern over the victim's situation is the focus, any verbal or nonverbal behaviors on the part of the suspected bully should be positively acknowledged if they even approach an expression of concern for the victim.

The intent of this first session is not interrogation intended to uncover the guilt of the suspected bully but rather to arrive at a common feeling of concern. Pikas advises that the interventionist should never overtly express the notion that "we share a common problem." Rather, he suggests that this is best conveyed nonverbally and through implication, such as through a concerned tone of voice. The keys to success in this endeavor are threefold. First, the adult maintains empathy with the victim's ordeal. Second, the interventionist conveys this solidarity with the victim to the bully. Third, the counselor conveys to the bully that, together, they will come to share a concern for the victim's plight.

If bullies deny knowledge of the harassment, interventionists should avoid engaging in a verbal power struggle regarding facts. While the innocence of the victim is assumed, this is no more than a best guess, a first hypothesis that is subject to revision. Instead of butting heads, the interventionist could change the topic to a relaxed discussion (in general terms) about relationships. Later, when the tenor of the meeting is more stable, the conversation could be returned to the victim's problems.

When strenuous denial of responsibility is encountered, it may be helpful to reenact and roleplay the event occasioning the referral. This could be framed as an attempt to achieve a clear perspective about the incident in question. The interventionist might volunteer to play the student's role after receiving permission from the student. The accuracy of the reenactment will be enhanced by the interventionist taking the time to be coached by the student concerning his or her own words and actions. This tactical procedure leaves the suspected bully in the position of playing the role of the alleged victim and presents an opportunity to further direct the experience toward a sharing of the related feelings generated by peer abuse. However, reverse role playing is a very complex procedure and will not work for everyone.

Points #3 & #4—Setting the Stage for Resolution. There are several factors that may help determine when the issue has been discussed sufficiently. First, it will likely take from 5 to 10 minutes to wrap up the session and schedule the needed follow-up visits. Second, the student's readiness to solve problems at point #4 should be weighed. Further opportunity to view the bullying from the victim's perspective may be needed. Arousal and energy levels may need to be heightened as an appropriate impetus for problem solving. The level of personal responsibility and problem ownership expressed by the bully, the readiness to look for answers, along with expressions of remorse are success indicators.

Another factor to consider is one of justice and fairness to the students. Have they been given ample opportunity to tell their story? The final consideration concerns the level of emotion that is present. As illustrated in Figure 7.1, the level of emotion should reach its apex at this time; with declining emotional arousal comes an increased likelihood that reasoning will be heard.

The question, "What do you suggest?" may need to be clarified, perhaps made more concrete for younger students. A precise way to phrase this would be, "What are you going to do the next time you see Paul?" or "What's going to happen then?"

At point #4, as the emotional arousal is given a constructive outlet, it is hoped that the student will offer suggestions for improving the victim's situation and promise to stop the bullying. Responsibility for finding a solution is turned over to the bully. The use of silence by the interventionist immediately following statement four is particularly important. Our cultural dislike and discomfort with silence in conversations, resulting in increasing levels of tension, provides a needed push toward resolution.

Point #5—Concluding the Interview. The statement at point #5 calls for additional comments. First, the reinforcing remark of "That's good" assumes that the student has indicated a willingness to address the problem and propose a solution. If resolution has not occurred, this fact must be verbalized for the sake of clarity. The student should be informed concerning the consequences of the situation in terms of school policy and procedures. If the student still has not reached a resolution, the interventionist can propose a parent-child conference to further consider the situation.

Concerning follow-up, a commonly used routine calls for a one-week interval between meetings to give time for change to occur. However, this will not be appropriate if the victim's safety remains in question or if the proposed solution is not realistic, complete, or mutually satisfactory. It would be better if the first session were not discontinued until a realistic, appropriate solution that assured the safety of the victim was achieved. However, this may not always be possible, and contingent plans may need to be fashioned.

Dealing With Non-Provocative Victims

Immediately after the interviews are completed with the suspected bully or bullies, a talk with the victim is in order. The victim will probably be cooperative, because when bullies return to the classroom, they will communicate, at least nonverbally, their relief in avoiding punishment.

The role of the interventionist during this session is primarily one of support. The message to be conveyed is concern for the scapegoat's status as a target for abuse and a genuine desire to help the person improve his or her quality of life. It is recommended that communication should similarly begin with open questions, such as "How are things going with you?" or with simple statements of fact, such as, "I've heard that you've been mistreated." These statements also assume a greater equality of relationship than do questions that are more directive and may imply that a superior/subordinate relationship exists.

At point #2 (see Fig. 7.2), the adult conveys information about precipitating or triggering events. For example, an incident may have started with remarks about the victim's body odor or something else that the student may be capable of changing. In such cases, victims are encouraged to work on problems, while still being provided the message that their victimization status is unfair.

At point #4 in the interview, the interventionist has to decide whether to continue responding to the victim's needs or to move the interview to point #5 and have a meeting arranged between the victim and the former bullies. The joint session with both bullies and victims is, after all, the final goal of this intervention. However, this goal does assume that a positive spirit on the part of all parties will be present during the joint session. Generating a spirit of cooperation between formerly warring parties is no small task. Expect the process to require a considerable expenditure of time and effort.

Pikas's Common Concern Method

FIGURE 7.2: THE CLASSIC VICTIM AND THE PROVOCATIVE VICTIM

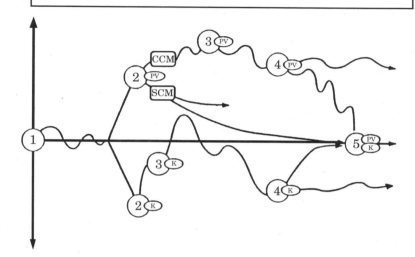

K = Kent, an example of the classic victim
PV = Peter V, an example of the provocative victim
CCM = Common Concern Method with PV
SCM = Suggestive Command Method with PV

Communication on the therapist's terms

Communication on equal terms between the therapist and the victim of mobbing

Communication on the victim's terms

Talking with Provocative Victims

The session with the provocative victim in many ways resembles the talk with the bully. That is, the troubling situation is discussed until the therapist and the provocative victim come to a mutual view of the situation. The interventionist's tone of voice during this part of the session is particularly important, because caring and concern are to be conveyed nonverbally. In addition, Pikas recommends that the counselor move events along swiftly.

At point #2, the person undertaking the CCM session decides whether to directly tell the provocative student that if he stops provoking others, the bullying will likely cease. An alternative practice is to introduce this notion with sufficient subtlety that the student takes ownership of the idea. One approach to planting the idea in "Peter's" mind that he may be provoking bullies is to help the student determine the provoking behavior's purpose, without labeling it as such. Dreikurs (1968) proposed the following goals for misbehavior that may be worth considering with the student:

1. Maladaptive behavior may be a way to declare inadequacy and signal withdrawal from social engagement.

2. Inappropriate responses may reflect an effort to seek revenge for an earlier slight or injustice.

3. A youngster may seek attention by means of actions that others find annoying.

4. A troubled adolescent may respond in ways that he or she feels will increase personal power.

Once a possible purpose for the provocative behavior is established, the interventionist explores more constructive alternatives. For example, the student may come to prefer gaining recognition by tutoring younger students or pursuing physical challenges, such as therapeutic ropes courses or Outward Bound. Floyd (1985) employs weight training with bully victims, reportedly with gratifying outcomes.

At point #3, the interventionist discovers that the provocative victim is willing to discuss alternate routes to popularity. The desire to be recognized and liked may be confirmed by the interventionist with the suggestion that the victim is simply going about it in the wrong way. At this point, the scapegoat is allowed to find more acceptable ways of achieving genuine and useful social approval and friendships.

At point #4, the interventionist considers whether changes induced in the provocative victim will make a socially valid difference. The provocative victim is informed that the counselor will meet the former bully, with the object of proposing a meeting of all parties. At this point, the counselor makes clear assurances regarding the victim's physical and psychological safety during the upcoming session. An interviewing checklist for use with provocative victims is included in the appendices (pp. 138–139).

The Group-Work Follow-up Option

After about a week, the talks described above are repeated in order to evaluate and highlight gains. The victim may or may not be included at this time depending on the responsible adult's best judgment. In the case of provocative victims, Pikas (1989b) advised holding group sessions; however, more time may be needed to coordinate the two sides. The purpose of the meeting is to work out mutually agreeable solutions to the bully-victim problem. The counselor may have to be quite persistent in returning to the question of what should be done.

The bully/victim session requires considerable preparation. An opportunity to teach responsibility may be introduced into the planning process by asking bullies for suggestions. What do they need to do? How might they best prepare for meeting with the victim? The same consideration is given to the victim. Occasionally, the person conducting the intervention will have to float a proposal. In that case, the following method is suggested: first, each bully will express in sincere and positive terms his or her opinion about the victim, who will be asked to listen during this time. Then the interventionist, as mediator, will ask the victim what he or she has to say about what was just heard. A positive response is a worthy first step.

Two precautions associated with group meetings are worth considering. First, the interventionist should continue in the mediator role, ensuring that students speak in the proper order, and avoid being drawn into the role of prosecutor or judge. A counselor placed in that role by participants can simply return the responsibility for solutions to student participants. Second, an effective practice is to be alert for the positive. The interventionist must attend to any change that heads in the proper direction, no matter how tenuous it is.

Before a group session is ended, it is helpful to ask, "What shall we do if somebody cannot keep the promises made?" It is suggested at this point that rather than the interventionist quickly agreeing to a penalty for failure to comply, the students briefly discuss the importance of tolerance and allowing room for mistakes. The message being conveyed through this discussion should be one of "let the other side live." A group session checklist is provided in the appendices (pp. 140–141).

Final Thoughts and Considerations

While we have gone to some detail in laying out this method for early intervention, this does not imply that one size fits all situations. In fact, the level of success to be found with the Common Concern Method will be proportional to the extent that the interventionist has individualized and tailored this approach to fit three important modifying factors. First, the needs and strengths of participants must be considered carefully. Second, CCM procedures may have to be altered in light of situational variables. Finally, individual differences, such as ethnic or racial background, may require modified procedures.

The time to develop relationships is not always realistically available. Thus CCM tends to prove more effective with pre-adolescents than with adolescents and in the early stages of the problem rather than in later stages. CCM, like many other forms of intervention, takes advantage of the fearlessness and greater malleability of the young, factors that tend to outweigh the gains in reasoning and abstract problem-solving capacities of adolescence.

Summary

- The role of the early intervention practitioner was discussed in terms of opening relational pathways.

- Practitioners were encouraged to examine their own personalities for factors that may reduce the effectiveness of the Common Concern Method, especially being aware of one's emotional triggers and need to control situations.

- The Common Concern Method (CCM) (Pikas, 1989b) was introduced as a structured five-stage, problem-solving model for guiding early intervention efforts with both victimized and bullying students. Empathy formation with the victim and its promotion in the bully/victim relationship was identified as the guiding principle and intent of the method when used with bullies.

- The CCM was viewed as useful for enhancing the personal empowerment of victimized students.

- In situations where victim provocations exacerbate bullying, practitioners may wish to consider the (sometimes hidden) purposes served by the victim's behavior.

- A group-work option was explored as a potent tool for monitoring progress, promoting additional problem-solving and problem-resolution work, and offering prospective reconciliation opportunities and the development of pathways for new lines of communication.

CHAPTER 8

INDIVIDUAL AND SMALL-GROUP INTERVENTION METHODS

While the Common Concern Method can be effective, other interventions are also needed for bully-victim situations. This chapter briefly examines other intervention strategies.

Readers should determine if these strategies fit their personal style. If the counselor does not feel comfortable with the strategy, he or she will not be able to use it effectively.

Five effective intervention strategies are introduced. These strategies will be considered in light of their application with both bullying and victimized students. Methods examined include reverse role playing, behavioral contracting, self-monitoring, and other cognitive modifications.

Strategies for Counseling and Intervention Work with Bullies

Reverse Role Playing

Reverse role playing (RRP) may be used as a tool for assessment, empathy training, and evaluation. It may also be used to explore and rehearse new behaviors.

As was noted in the discussion of the CCM, reverse role playing is frequently helpful in the first interview as a means of furthering the understanding of all parties concerning the nature of a harassment episode. It is particularly suited for work with concrete thinkers, because it makes the incident visible. The beauty of RRP is that it not only helps the assessment of the situation, it also furthers the goal of developing empathy.

Before reversing roles, set the stage for RRP by role playing the event, with the bully enacting his or her own part and the interventionist assuming the role of the victimized student. During reenactments, the practitioner clarifies the thinking of the bully about the events that elicited the behavior. For example, the interventionist may interrupt the scene to ask, "What were you thinking when you first approached Donny?" or "What did the others around you do when you first called Donny a wimp?" Questions of this nature should generate useful information about antecedent events, anticipated consequences, and contextual factors. This information then can be put to work in designing interventions.

After sufficient clarification has been attained, the role reversal can be initiated. First, the interventionist explains the reason for trying a reverse role play and provides a brief summary of procedures. It might be pointed out that RRP will provide an opportunity to demonstrate exactly what happened rather than simply talk about it.

Once cooperation is procured, the bully is asked to relate all he or she knows about the scapegoated student. In addition, the bully is asked to carefully describe the circumstances surrounding the scene. The bully is actually empowered to work his or her way out of the problem situation by being asked to lead the initial discussion. The bully is encouraged to fully assume the role of victim and play it to the hilt, to replicate the scapegoat's tone of voice, habits, and mannerisms. While the enactment may come to resemble a mocking caricature of the victimized student, it is generally assumed that the more lifelike the portrayal, the better (Ivey, 1988).

Typically, at least 5 to 10 minutes of role play is suggested. However, if the experience proves particularly powerful or instructive, more time may be allocated. The reenactment's ending should be clearly identified. Next, the experience is discussed in detail to further enhance the effect. A brief summary of the total experience by the interventionist will help confirm the story. If agreement is not reached about how the victim experienced the event, it may be necessary to review, or even reenact, critical incidents.

Behavioral Contracting

Behavioral or contingency contracting is a proven way to consolidate agreements forged in counseling sessions or in conflict-resolution negotiations. Contingency contracts are documents that spell out specific behaviors of participants. The more clearly the behavior is stated, the more effective the contract arrangement will be. As a sign of good faith, all parties sign and date the contractual document (Alberto & Troutman, 1995). An excellent pamphlet is available by Hall & Hall (1982) detailing the nuts and bolts of negotiating contingency contracts.

The behavior of former bullies spelled out in a behavioral contract must include a promise to refrain from bullying and a publicly observable definition of which behaviors constitute bullying. Some experts recommend that contracts be stated positively. Thus, in the case of both bullies and victims, wording about prosocial behavior could be added.

The contracts of victims might include such items as ignoring teasing, giving carefully defined assertive responses, and improving behaviors that others see as provocative and that the former scapegoat also wishes to alter. The behavior of the helping professional is specified on behavioral contracts and generally consists of the contingent delivery of a reward.

Perhaps the most beneficial aspect of contracting in the case of bullying is that the process of negotiation itself is propitious. In negotiating with a student, a teacher or counselor models the type of problem-solving behavior that should ameliorate bullying problems. In addition, the helper is engaged in a very egalitarian relationship. In defining behaviors that have proved problematic, the counselor and student have already completed part of the task of coming to understand bullying (or a lack of assertion) and the difficulties these patterns engender.

The Winning Ticket

The "Winning Ticket" is a simple incentive system or token economy for helping students learn how to control aggressive behaviors by focusing on positive goals. Floyd (1985) noted that the Winning Ticket method helps students discern that positive behavior can be more rewarding than antisocial responses.

Each student is scored on ten selected, positively framed skills for each period of the school day with a maximum score per day of 100. While Floyd does make allowance for scoring before-school and lunch-time behaviors, he omits the scoring of after-school behavior as impractical. However, as most bullying behavior occurs out of the classroom (Hazler, Hoover, & Oliver, 1991), we would suggest that a system for monitoring and documenting after-school behavior be included if possible. Practitioners should develop goals and behavioral indicators specific to the unique needs of each student.

Floyd recommends that students must achieve a score of at least 85 for the day to receive a token. Fourteen tokens are required for the reward, for example, a free lunch at a fast-food restaurant. Each child is held responsible for returning his or her Winning Ticket each day with a parent's signature. This procedure keeps the parents informed and better involved in the child's progress on a daily basis. The Winning Ticket thus serves as a daily report card on the student's progress toward needed growth and changes.

Self-Monitoring

Self-monitoring involves putting the student in charge of his or her own behavior. One version of this would be to have bullies tally aggressive words or actions that discount others' rights, such as name-calling or pushing. A more positive method is to have the student record positive, prosocial responses. For example, a student could record periods of time in which she engaged in selected positive behaviors, such as greeting others. A similar method is to teach the student to record the passage of time intervals during which targeted bullying behaviors did not occur (Alberto & Troutman, 1995).

A central feature of self-monitoring is that the child must learn to identify both inappropriate behaviors (for example, bullying) and appropriate responses. This "educative" component may be as important for the success of self-monitoring as is attending to one's own behavior. It also fits well with the various "talk counseling" models that have been discussed.

Rehearsal and Imagery Techniques

Behavioral rehearsal and associated imagery techniques have been shown to work with children of widely varying ages and in many different situations. As with other behavioral methods discussed, the principles involved are straightforward. First, imaging must be practiced and feedback provided if students are to learn the procedure well enough for imaging to be useful. Second, both overt practice of the targeted adaptive behavior and covert rehearsal of images of the response are necessary.

It is of particular importance to encourage students to consider the effect of new, adaptive response modalities on peers. This might be framed with questions, such as: "What is this going to mean to your friends and classmates?" or "What will be different and what will be the same at school after these changes are made?" Also have the student consider what he or she will do in several settings. For example, you might ask the student to consider, "What would it be like now if you encountered Melissa before school in the hall?" Students must be rewarded by practitioners for practicing their responses until their improved behavior generates natural reinforcers in the form of more pleasing interactions with others and successful problem resolution. The following steps are suggested for guiding students' use of imagery in interpersonal problem solving:

1. Generate specific alternatives to the responses that have brought the student to the attention of authorities. This part of the process is similar to the notion of brainstorming.

2. Review the alternatives calmly and rationally.

3. Evaluate the alternatives. The counselor may need to assist the student to develop criteria with which to judge a strategy.

4. Select one or more of the alternatives, based on step 3, and plan implementation of the strategies.

5. Practice overtly (that is, the response alternative) and covertly (that is, the images of using the new skill in different settings).

Strategies for Counseling and Intervention Work with Scapegoats

The procedures for counseling bullies discussed above also apply to victims. Reverse role playing may allow the chronic scapegoat to better understand how his or her behavior appears to others. Behavioral contracting and self-monitoring may be used in a behavior-change plan. Similarly, imagery techniques may be used to further needed changes identified by victimized students and their adult helpers. This might prove especially helpful for rehearsing new ways of interacting with others, particularly harassing students. This seems most appropriate if aggressive or provoking behaviors on the part of the scapegoat are present.

Four additional strategies are directly applicable to individual counseling with victims. Assertiveness training, social skills training, planning for strength building, and cognitive strategies are described below.

Assertiveness Training

Assertiveness may be defined as standing up for one's rights while not trampling on the rights of others (Alberti & Emmons, 1982; Bellack & Hersen, 1977). Identification, clarification, and affirmation of one's rights are central to effective intervention. Scapegoats are reminded repeatedly that they possess the right to say no to bullying and that there are ways to do this without suffering abuse.

A rule taken from parent education applies in this case: "Say what you mean and mean what you say." Learning this rule thoroughly helps youngsters to set limits on what they will put up with.

Victimized students also must be made aware that anticipation and avoidance of humiliating encounters is often a legitimate coping strategy. Most chronic victims will be way ahead of you on this one! Nonetheless, issues of guilt and embarrassment often arise and must be handled sensitively by the helping adult. A related concept is that teens and pre-teens must learn to leave the scene of a confrontation with dignity.

These core elements and the associated assertive behaviors are taught primarily through the use of modeling over approximately seven 45-minute sessions. One feature of a successful bullying prevention and reduction program is that helping adults model assertive actions while avoiding aggressive behavior.

The effectiveness of assertiveness training may also be enhanced by the use of imagery techniques. There are many creative ways to incorporate imagery throughout the process. For example, the practitioner might ask students to imagine what it would look and feel like to assertively ask a bully to stop poking them.

Five key steps are involved in assertiveness training:

1. Identify the problem situation.

2. Identify the needed changes and new behaviors.

3. Practice and refine the new behaviors.

4. Plan and apply the new behaviors.

5. Evaluate and make changes as needed.

In step 1, the student and interventionist identify the persons involved and the problem situations and circumstances where the harassment occurs. These are ranked in terms of their difficulty for the student to handle, from most threatening to least threatening. In cases where the pain of recounting these scenes may be troubling, relaxation training could be added to the assertiveness lessons.

Both the words and actions that the student displays during abusive encounters are discussed, and any needed changes are considered during step 2. This is a delicate step, as the victim should in no way be blamed. Depending on the age of the student, the counselor might simply ask, "What may be a better way to act at that time?" or "What might be a better way for you to deal with the situation, should that happen again sometime?" This line of inquiry is preferred to the more customarily used negative framing of, "Is there anything that you are doing in the given situation that may in any way be making the situation worse?"

After alternatives are evaluated, the student systematically practices the new behaviors, starting with the least difficult situation. In individual work, the counselor should first model the behavior by playing the role of the victimized student; effective modeling procedes as follows:

1. Model verbal responses in a clear and detailed manner.

2. Demonstrations proceed from least to most difficult behaviors to be undertaken by the learner.

3. Modeling should be repeated frequently enough to facilitate thorough learning.

4. Avoid presenting irrelevant details.

5. Employ several different individuals to model behaviors; especially helpful are persons who share pertinent characteristics with the learner (Goldstein et al., 1980).

Following the modeling of new behavior, the helping professional assumes the harasser role as the student practices newly learned adaptive responses. In cases where assertiveness training is undertaken in groups, other members of the group participate in the enactment.

The facilitator must ensure that responses are enacted as realistically as possible. Nonverbal factors, such as facial expression, vocal tone, and posturing, carry the majority of the message; these components must be considered carefully. Congruence between words and nonverbal messages is required for effective communication of assertiveness.

Assertiveness training requires both planning and applying the new behavior in real-life situations. The planning should include provisions for rewarding correct performance of assertive responses. The student can deliver self-reinforcement, or the facilitator, teachers, or parents could do so.

The facilitator of assertiveness training should encourage the learner to keep a journal and should provide necessary instructions. Times and places where the assertive responses are employed and the results of standing up for one's rights are recorded carefully. The learner should be reminded that instant success is not to be expected. Adults in the child's environment should provide much-needed support during this vulnerable period.

The last step is to jointly evaluate the results of assertiveness training with the student. Modifications in assertive scripts could be developed in light of the critique.

Once the least difficult behavior has been used successfully, the trainer should then methodically move the student toward practicing the response in the next, more difficult situation. This procedure continues until assertive responses have been made for all problematic situations.

Social Skills Training

In surveys of the characteristics perceived by students to motivate bullying (Hoover, Oliver, & Hazler, 1992), the seven items rated highest by both sexes were "didn't fit in" (the most frequent reason given for bullying by both sexes), "physically weak," "I cried/was emotional," "short tempered," "facial appearance," "who my friends were," and "the clothes I wore." The leading perceived motivator, as well as four of the seven most frequent answers, may be said to fall under the heading of social skills.

Of course, it must be kept firmly in mind that students may be left out of a school's social life through no fault of their own—that is, despite possessing excellent social understanding. The environment, not the child, is often "sick." In *Reviving Ophelia,* Mary Pipher (1994) enumerates situation after situation where adolescent females are harassed for behaviors which in adults may be seen as eminently adaptive. For example, in one situation, a troubled teen discovers that her love for books is systematically denigrated by her peers, because in that particular environment, reading was considered "nerdy." Schools should be remolded into tolerant places where a wide range of mannerisms are accepted—even some that may be seen as odd.

The push-button technique is a useful method for students who are abused because they have more emotional "ups and downs" than others (Mosak, 1989). Push-button involves having students visualize alternately pleasant and unpleasant experiences, such as their most recent experience of crying at school in connection with harassment. After asking the student to recall the pleasant or happy experience, the helper equates happy scenes with pushing one's happy button. Unhappy experiences are compared to pressing the crying button. Sufficient time should be allotted for each experience to be fully felt by the student. Students are led to an understanding of feelings that accompany happy and unhappy scenes, with the aim of teaching them that thoughts contribute to feelings.

For the student with a "short temper," the implied social skill to learn is "anger management" (Eggert, 1994). In this procedure, the hot buttons that set the student off are identified and discussed. Following this, the student is taught that, in the future, these hot buttons will signal him or her to take a brief time out before saying or doing anything. Such methods as counting to 10 or backwards from 100, or even physically removing oneself from the encounter to briefly cool off and plan the new response, are taught. Alternate prosocial responses should then be developed as substitutes.

Other social skills that may be needed by victimized students include conflict resolution, negotiation, and simple courtesy. There are a number of good curricula already available that the interventionist or counselor may wish to use. Highly recommended helpful ideas can be found in the following works: *Creative Conflict Resolution: More Than 200 Activities for Keeping Peace in the Classroom, K–6* (Kreidler, 1984); *Why Is Everybody Always Picking on Me? A Guide to Understanding Bullies* (Webster-Doyle, 1991). A more complete list of resources is provided in the appendices (pp. 145–148).

Planning for Strength Building

Victimized children tend to be physically weaker than average; this appears to consistently elicit aggression. As a result, increasing strength and athletic ability may decrease the risk of peer abuse. The key in these efforts is to work for small gains that nurture self-confidence. In time, the student's own interest and commitment must develop to successfully fuel this process; however, mentors may further this new learning by positively reinforcing all gains made by the student throughout the program of strength building. It is extremely important that weight training not be seen as preparatory to a physical conflict. Rather, positive effects probably result from an increased air of confidence and self-esteem. Nathaniel Floyd (1985), in his anti-bullying work, supports this strategy; he also believes that self-defense and martial arts programs hold promise.

Cognitive Methods and Strategies

These above strategies involve an array of counseling and teaching possibilities most suited to late middle school and early adolescence. Slightly older students are better candidates for "thinking-based" approaches, because these students possess the necessary level of cognitive sophistication. In cognitive training, change is fostered through a three-phase process, including attending to one's own responses, initiating improved internal dialogues and learning better coping skills.

For example, the self-monitoring described earlier is expanded to include teaching victims to listen to themselves, to their thoughts, feelings, actions, and physiological signs. The latter include such important stress indicators as breathing and heart rate. The students are encouraged to consider whether their thinking involves any of the following basic mistakes identified by Mosak (1989):

1. Overgeneralizations: for example, "The world is no good," or "Nobody cares anything about me."

2. False or impossible goals: for example, "I must please everyone around me if I am to be loved or cared about."

3. Misperceptions of life and life's demands: "Nothing ever works out for me. Life has doomed me from the start."

4. Denial of basic worth: "I'm just not as good as everyone else; why should anyone care?"

5. Faulty values: "Only winning counts; everything else is just second best."

Counselors deliver the message that behavioral "mistakes" are really "thinking" mistakes that are readily correctable. Students often require reassurance that they can bring their troublesome behavior under control and that requisite skills are within their grasp.

In the second phase, starting new internal dialogues and self-talk, the student is directed toward self-affirming thoughts and actions. For example, for the frequently observed belief of victims that they "don't fit in," students are helped to recognize this erroneous inner message, question its truth, and learn to substitute an affirmation.

The final phase of this strategy consists of teaching students effective coping skills. These skills are identified, rehearsed in role plays, and ultimately practiced in real life. For example, if the student is afraid he will not make the football team, the teacher or helper may help him with changing his negative view of failure, thereby making him more willing to engage in the desired activity. The student then continues to tell himself new sentences and subsequently observe and assess the outcomes of these altered thoughts. As the student starts to act differently, he usually gets new reactions from others. Again, what students say to themselves about their new coping behaviors and their consequences is significant (see Meichenbaum, 1977; 1985; 1986; McMullin, 1986).

As the last phase is of crucial importance, we want to spell out the five-step procedure used to teach these coping skills:

1. Expose the student, through role-play and imagery exercises, to the anxiety-provoking situations that trouble them.

2. Teach the student how to rate their discomfort and anxiety on a scale of 1 to 10.

3. Teach former victims how to become aware of the thoughts and beliefs they experience in stressful situations.

4. Encourage the student to reevaluate and correct his or her self-talk, and teach the skills for doing so.

5. Have the student note the level of discomfort (anxiety) that follows this reevaluation.

These coping skills may also be used in conjunction with stress inoculation training (Corey, 1991). In this method, the student is given chances to deal successfully with relatively mild stress-invoking stimuli, so that he or she gradually develops a tolerance for stronger stimuli. Problem solving, relaxation training, behavioral rehearsals, self-monitoring, self-instruction and reinforcement, and modifying environmental situations all may be used by the helping professional in this type of exercise. The behavioral version of this method is called systematic desensitization (Wolpe, 1990).

In general, coping-skills training and stress inoculation training should prove especially useful in dealing with victimized children and adolescents with difficulties involving speech anxieties, social withdrawal, and social incompetence. It is probably most effective when used in conjunction with a program of social skills training.

The Narrative or Restorying Strategy

The retelling strategy described here combines elements drawn from the Adlerian mutual storytelling technique (see Kottman & Stiles, 1990) and the narrative approach to family counseling detailed in White and Epston (1990). This technique involves treating one's life as a story and then "rewriting" the ending to reflect the desired outcomes.

The retelling strategy is most compatible with non-Western outlooks on conflict resolution. Many Native American, Central American, and Eastern cultures see conflict primarily as circular, rather than linear. As a story traces a circle from rest in the beginning to conflict and back to rest, so conflict mimics this form (Auruch, Black, & Scimicca, 1991).

The fundamental assumption in this approach is that a person's relations with others are analogous to telling the story of his or her experience. It is through telling one's own story and, in turn, being told the story of another that we determine the meaning given to our existence. In the process of retelling their stories, people enter into their story, take it over, and make it more fully theirs. The evolution of their life then involves the repeated telling and retelling of their story. This retelling involves reinterpretation, with the result that victims can retell their story with a happier ending.

The five basic steps in applying the retelling strategy are discussed below.

1. Hearing the Child's Story

The helping adult encourages the child to tell his or her own story. Part of that story will concern either harassment of another or his or her victimization. The helping adult listens to the story of other aspects of the child's life to determine whether the harassment or victimization fits or does not fit with the story of how the child sees himself or herself.

2. Identifying Unique Outcomes

These are the exceptions to the behavior or problem pattern that may be arrived at through such questions as: "What other ways besides bullying does the child use to solve his or her problems?"; "How does the child treat others when he or she is not engaged in hostile behavior?"; and "What actions does the student show that are incompatible with the role of the bully (or victim)?"

3. Externalizing the Problem

Externalizing means objectifying a problem situation so that it can be talked about. It is particularly important to clarify with students the relationship between a problem situation and their previous attempts to resolve it.

4. Weaving a New Story

Weaving refers to bringing together all the elements of the child's story so that it accounts for both the unique outcomes and the possible resolutions to the problem. This allows the events of the story to be explained and thus resolved. The counselor also should encourage use of the "I" pronoun by the student to promote personal responsibility for the narrative. This is also the stage at which the child is encouraged to change his or her story.

5. Sharing the New Story and Promoting the Change

The idea at this step is to encourage and support the new story arrived at in the last step. It presents an opportunity for the child to help others get to know him or her better. One way of fostering success with the last step is to plan the best time and place for sharing the story. The helping adult can gauge the child's readiness for doing this by asking questions and getting to the details of when, where, and with whom they plan to share their new understanding.

Journal Writing as an Adjunct Activity

Keeping a journal can be a helpful tool for leading the student through the storying process. The journal can be written in a dialogue format, with the counselor writing short comments about what the child has written. This form of written dialogue requires clear permission from the child for the counselor to read the journal.

Case Illustration of the Restorying Method

The entire process of restorying may best be explained by providing an example. The adolescent student in this case dreaded presenting orally in class. Her peers teased her about her reticence, so she viewed the assignment with considerable trepidation. The young lady had a history of victimization, both in male-female relationships and from bullying. Her problems may have been exacerbated by the interaction of her Native American heritage with the larger Anglo culture of the school.

She spoke of being awkwardly and excessively shy, particularly in front of others at school. When asked to tell about how it all began, she related a story of visiting her mother's sister's home as a young child and spending an evening playing with her aunt's children behind a large wood-burning stove. She explained that her father had left the family at about that time, seemingly for good, and that her mother had gone out for the evening. With continually increasing pace, she related that her mother came in very late, staggering and loudly demanding to know her daughter's whereabouts. The girl's aunt tried to get her mother to go home, saying the child was asleep and that the aunt would bring her over the next morning. She remembered feeling very shy and frightened at the time and was glad she wouldn't be going out in the cold. As a result, she pretended to be asleep while her mother looked for her. The girl's mother was finally persuaded by her "other mother" to leave without the child. Being still and quiet had worked. The story ended with her voicing a fondness for her aunt's loving protectiveness.

On reflection, it seemed that her life since the time represented in the narrative was consistent—the story was one of hiding and pretending not to be there, of making herself small and seemingly invisible. After recognizing this thread, the counselor helped the young woman seek occasions when she stepped forward and came out of hiding, when she spoke her mind in front of others, times when her voice was clear and strong. A new story was slowly pieced together, describing a journey from pensive concealment to coming out of hiding, of speaking out with her own authentic, clear voice.

This restorying change was supplemented and reinforced by having the counselor ask about the stories from her culture where women spoke up for themselves and led. Much mutual learning and recognition of strengths followed. The student came to know her voice as a gift to be used. This seemed to make it much easier for her to transfer this learning to performance in the classroom.

Summary

- Both role playing (RP) and reverse role playing (RRP) techniques may be incorporated in the CCM. Use of RP and RRP for assessment and empathy-building purposes was discussed.

- Reverse role playing involves teaching bullies to depict the behavior of scapegoats. In working with victims, the process is reversed. By playing the other's role, the student may come to understand the dynamics of problem situations.

- Behavioral contracting refers to an agreement between either bullies or victims and a facilitator. The bully agrees to refrain from aggression and the helping professional agrees to provide a reward. Whipping boys and girls can contract to demonstrate increased levels of assertion.

- Self-monitoring is a strategy whereby troubled students can be taught to attend to their own problem or adaptive behaviors, thereby decreasing the former and increasing the latter.

- It may assist bullies to reduce aggression if they are taught to imagine adaptive responses and to rehearse them mentally.

- Ways in which assertiveness training might be utilized in teaching alternative communication modes during confrontations were explored. Suggestions for the use of relaxation training, teaching how to leave the scene of confrontation with dignity, and the use of constructive avoidance were also explored as means of enhancing assertion training.

- Social skills training was found to be an effective strategy for addressing and combatting the factors motivating bullying. In a skills approach, problems are attributed to a lack of knowledge about actions rather than to pathology. Students learn to emit new, more adaptive responses with the help of teachers.

- The push-button technique was advised for use with overly emotive victims. This involves using the imagery of a button to code arousal-inducing and pleasure-enhancing stimuli.

- Strength building and associated disciplines were suggested as courses of action for the teacher or interventionist to either employ or support. It is important that these are seen as confidence builders, not preparation for the big fight.

- Cognitive strategies are helpful for controlling fears, managing stress, and teaching new coping skills to victims. They were noted to be particularly effective in cases of social withdrawal and incompetence. Cognitive training involves teaching children to "talk to themselves inside" in more adaptive ways.

CHAPTER

9

USING BIBLIOTHERAPY TO REDUCE BULLYING

Stories have power. Stories are tied to the imagination, and it is in this wonderful place that hope lives. In reading about another student facing the same plight, a chronic victim may derive comfort or, better yet, learn a new coping idea. The bully might begin to identify with a bullied character, thus leading to empathy—a necessary resource for change (Pikas, 1989a).

We looked at children's books published over the past fifteen years, with a focus on the middle school reader, and found that they have much to say that both bullies and victims need to hear—stories about coping, enduring, and overcoming. They describe insights reached, patterns of problem solving, and many lessons in nonviolent alternatives to fighting that kids need to know. In short, stories offer a rainbow of perspectives that may prove invaluable to children and to those who care about them.

We found that stories addressing bullying also contained some messages that should be dealt with cautiously. For example, the climax might be a brutal fight followed by a denouement where the hero learns the value of physical violence. Most experts in the field eschew this approach. The message here is that bibliotherapy, as is true of all approaches to the problem of bullying, must be handled judiciously by teachers.

Coping Skills and Strategies

A systematic approach was taken to identify coping strategies in children's books. First, we searched the World Catalog Index (WorldCat) of the FirstSearch database, using "bullies" and "bullying" as descriptors. Forty-three books were identified. These were examined for bullying solutions, and strategies were categorized (Oliver, Young, & LaSalle, 1994).

Contrary to the advice provided by experts on aggression, the solution most often portrayed in these stories was revenge, often including heavy doses of violence. These books are listed in the following tables. Table 9.1 lists books with short-term coping strategies; Table 9.2 consists of ten conflict resolution strategies.

TABLE 9.1: BOOKS EXEMPLIFYING SHORT-TERM COPING STRATEGIES

Strategies	Books*
Avoidance and ignoring the problem	*Hang on, Harvey!; Courage at Indian Deep; The Present Takers; The Revenge of the Incredible Dr. Rancid and His Youthful Assistant, Jeffrey; What a Wimp; Rafa's Dog; Make Me a Hero; The Hopscotch Tree*
Use of distraction and confusion	*Courage at Indian Deep*
Acting as if bullying gesture is not intended as a bullying gesture	*There's a Boy in the Girl's Bathroom*
Imagining success with the problem and writing a story about it**	*The Revenge of the Incredible Dr. Rancid and His Youthful Assistant, Jeffrey*
Being escorted to and from school and protected by an older sibling	*What a Wimp*
Increasing conformity in actions and dress to group expectations	*The Kid with the Red Suspenders*
Attempts to embarrass and/or humiliate the bully**	*One Thing for Sure; The Present Takers; Ghosts in the Fourth Grade*
Use of humor	*Courage at Indian Deep; Wilted; Hang on, Harvey!; The Revenge of the Incredible Dr. Rancid and His Youthful Assistant, Jeffrey; The Boy Who Lost His Face*
Acting "as if" unafraid	*The Boy Who Lost His Face*
Using a dog for protection	*Courage at Indian Deep*
Avoiding labeling as the "teacher's pet" by making a pact with the teacher to avoid public praise	*The Kid with the Red Suspenders*
Imagining someone else suffering greater misery	*The Boy Who Lost His Face*

*Not all books may currently be in print.
**Both short-term and long-term strategy.

TABLE 9.2: BOOKS EXEMPLIFYING CONFLICT RESOLUTION STRATEGIES

Strategies	Books*
Shared experience of adversity between bully and victim	*Courage at Indian Deep; Stepping on the Cracks; The Hopscotch Tree; Gopher Takes Heart*
Gaining new competencies that are respected by the peer group	*Courage at Indian Deep; Make Me a Hero*
Being empowered by being given new and respected responsibilities	*What a Wimp; Make Me a Hero; The Kid with the Red Suspenders; The Hopscotch Tree; Gopher Takes Heart*
Gaining increased independence from an overly protective family	*The Kid with the Red Suspenders*
Photographing the bully in a compromising situation and using threat of public exposure to end harassment	*One Thing for Sure*
Verbal confrontation only	*What a Wimp; The Present Takers; There's a Boy in the Girl's Bathroom; The Once in a While Hero; The Hopscotch Tree*
Gaining a philosophical perspective that increases empathy with, and understanding of, the perpetrator	*Wilted; Stepping on the Cracks; A Bundle of Sticks; The Revenge of the Incredible Dr. Rancid and His Youthful Assistant, Jeffrey; Tough Beans; The Hopscotch Tree*
Making friends/negotiating peace	*There's a Boy in the Girl's Bathroom; Make Me a Hero; Stepping on the Cracks; Gopher Takes Heart*
Gaining physical strength and learning fighting skills	*Stepping on the Cracks; Popcorn*
Fighting	*Hang on, Harvey!; The Revenge of the Incredible Dr. Rancid and His Youthful Assistant, Jeffrey; The Boy Who Lost His Face; Wilted; Rafa's Dog; Stepping on the Cracks*

*Not all books may currently be in print.

Revenge as the Answer for Bullying

Revenge was offered as the resolution strategy in nearly one-third of available books (7/22). In these selections, the story tended to revolve around diminutive, weak boys who were victimized repeatedly by more physically adroit youngsters. Bullies tended to be portrayed as tough-minded and merciless. Unfair matches, such as those developed by the writers, do match what is known about bullying. Unsuccessful attempts to avoid or elude the tormentor are chronicled; a day of reckoning typically arrives. The conclusion in each case is that "standing up" to the bully is the only alternative. The story usually ends with the victim scarred but renewed with self-confidence.

A story that is a prototype for the revenge motif is *The Boy Who Lost His Face* (Sacher, 1989). An elderly woman is taunted for practicing witchcraft; ultimately, her cane is stolen by a gang of neighborhood boys. David's need to belong motivates the protagonist to join the gang. He is troubled with guilt and, in the end, concludes that if you don't stand up for yourself, you disgracefully lose face before all. So David winds up tangling with the bully and regains his face in the process, even though it's now mostly black and blue. Other children's books showing revenge themes in a positive light include: *Hang on, Harvey!* (Hopper, 1984); *The Revenge of the Incredible Dr. Rancid and His Youthful Assistant, Jeffrey* (Conford, 1980); *The Once in a While Hero* (Adler, 1982); *Wilted* (Kropp, 1980); *Rafa's Dog* (Griffiths, 1983); *A Bundle of Sticks* (Mauser, 1982).

Imagination and Pretense

Four of twelve authors employed the use of imagination to solve their characters' bullying problems. In one solution, the character acted as if he was unafraid during all instances when the tormentor was present (Sacher, 1989); a variation on this theme is acting as if the bully were not present at all and that the bullying did not occur (Sacher, 1989). In the latter case, the reader is given an example of reattribution—of reinterpreting the intent of the bullying behavior as positive or benign and then going about one's business unperturbed and unannoyed.

Another use of imagination for coping is keeping in mind the picture of a soul so profoundly miserable that the protagonist's travails with bullying pale to insignificance. It is easy to see how imagined calamities might offer comfort, at least to a degree; but it may not be the type of humanistic regard for others that we wish to encourage. Also, it is not realistic to ask children with limited experiences and world views to downplay their own suffering in the context of others' misfortunes.

Perhaps the children's book most deserving of an award for constructive use of imagination would be Conford's story, *The Revenge of the Incredible Dr. Rancid and His Youthful Assistant, Jeffrey.* The young protagonist is trapped in a victimizing pattern of peer abuse. Jeffrey responds, however, by imagining a successful outcome to the torment, writing a story about it, and then recalling the triumphant moments in times of despair and defeat. It comes across as a self-empowering strategy which keeps hope alive, even though Jeffrey's imagined solution conjured up superhuman powers. This approach to bullying is reminiscent of the principle of "acting as if," wherein children imagine ways of behaving and then role play them.

Finding Protectors and the Humor in Situations

Two other strategies that deserve further comment include finding allies to serve as protectors and using humor to cope. Protectors varied from an older brother to a large dog. In *What a Wimp* (Carrick, 1982), an older brother escorts a bullying victim to and from school. In *Courage at Indian Deep* (Thomas, 1984), a loyal dog serves as the guardian.

One may perform a humorous act to defuse a stressful encounter. As humor may be unexpected at such times, it can serve to alter the pace of events and thus serve as a distraction. For example, the protagonist's little sister spills her box of Skittles at the big showdown with the bully in the book *Courage at Indian Deep*. Specific suggestions for employing humor to defuse bullying episodes are offered in Webster-Doyle's *Why Is Everybody Always Picking on Me? A Guide to Understanding Bullies for Young People* (1991).

Problem Resolution Strategies

While ten separate strategies are listed in Table 9.2, close examination reveals ideological connections between several of them. For example, the strategies of "Gaining new competencies that are respected by the peer group" is similar to the strategy of "Being empowered by being given new and respected responsibilities." Both are strategies related to competence. Empowerment motifs also are implied by the strategy of "Gaining increased independence from an overly-protective family." Independence is conceptually related to competence because it implies becoming more assertive in the relationships with the family. This same theme of victim empowerment appears in two other strategies found in fictive works, namely, "Gaining physical strength and learning fighting skills" and "Fighting."

Empowerment and Competence

Empowerment is played out in *Courage at Indian Deep* as the hero dispels the victim role by gaining highly respected woodcraft skills. By contrast, *Make Me a Hero* (Brooks, 1980) is an urban survival story where the necessary learning includes working at a trade and learning to negotiate and survive the streets. In these two books, empowerment is something you gain on your own and through individual effort. However, farther along the continuum, there are stories where the empowerment is gained from others. For example, teachers play a critical role in bestowing or sharing power, mainly through assigning special tasks or giving special privileges to the victimized children, as described in *The Hopscotch Tree* (Siskind, 1992) and *Gopher Takes Heart* (Scribner, 1993).

Another theme appearing in pre-adolescent fiction is that of gaining the empathy and understanding of the bully and moving beyond adversarial relationships. This focus is found in "Shared experience of adversity between bully and victim," "Gaining a philosophical perspective that increases empathy with, and understanding of, the perpetrator," and "Making friends/negotiating peace."

Using Books and Stories as Bibliotherapy

The potential educational and therapeutic benefits to be derived from literature are becoming increasingly accepted. Many case studies have been published in support of bibliotherapy (Riordan & Wilson, 1989; Schrank & Engels, 1981).

Several sources are available if the reader desires to dig deeper into bibliotherapeutic methods. The following volumes should prove helpful: *Books to Help Children Cope with*

Separation and Loss (Vol. 3, Bernstein & Rudman, 1989), *The Use of Enchantment* (Bettelheim, 1976), *Therapeutic Metaphor* (Gordon, 1978), *Therapeutic Metaphors for Children* (Mills & Crowley, 1986), and *Narrative Means to Therapeutic Ends* (White & Epston, 1990).

Classic Bibliotherapy: The Three-Stage Process

The most accepted and commonly held understanding of the therapeutic benefits of literature asserts that they are derived from a three-stage process. The first stage revolves around the process of identification by the reader with the central character in the story. The second stage is directed toward arriving at insight into the thoughts, feelings, and actions taken in relation to the problems, barriers, and dilemmas encountered in the story line. In other words, the reader comes to make knowledge connections and therefore to know one's self better and to understand the world better. The insight stage may be particularly difficult for young children. The third stage is one of emotional catharsis and release.

One could enhance the identification process by locating books that parallel the lives of troubled students. Practitioners move beyond mere matching of life situations by posing questions requiring comparisons with characters in the story.

In *One Thing for Sure* (Gifaldi, 1986), the protagonist, Pat, is shamed into questioning his masculinity. Such an emotionally potent question may be viewed as too threatening to utter openly on a first-person basis. However, when it is Pat that is asking the question, the matter might appear much safer. Once the association is made, options may be opened by asking questions similar to the following example: "If Pat were in this room right now, what would you tell him about what it means to be a man?" This type of indirect question is probably more effective than mere telling. It also matches with student-centered, discovery approaches to learning.

Group Guidance Applications

The process of bibliotherapy also can be merged into group guidance activities. For example, after a book has been read to students, the helping professional might work with the whole class by leading a discussion of the causes and effects of the bully's actions and the victim's responses (see Greenbaum, Turner, & Stephens, 1989). Useful questions might include, "What might cause a bullying student to act that way?" or "How would you feel and what would you do if you were treated that way by some bully?" Nonviolent coping strategies could be sought during a brainstorming session.

Students might be asked to select their favorite response from the brainstorming activity. An option is to allow students to suggest the best course of action for the fictional scapegoat and then rewrite the story's ending.

Another group activity using bibliotherapy is to help students act out the story. Crucial scenes and encounters might be highlighted for the learning opportunities they represent. If both bullying and victimized students are members of the class, then the teacher may wish to reverse the roles in order to provide possibilities for empathy to grow. Facilitators should allow time for a follow-up discussion of what was learned from the dramatic exercise.

Summary

- Coping skills and strategies may helpfully be divided in terms of whether they address only immediate situations and circumstances or whether they may also lead to long-term problem resolution.

- In recent children's books, story lines frequently revolve around revenge and retribution. These books tend to convey the message that it is often fruitful to answer violence in kind. This perspective is in opposition to expert recommendations.

- The coping and problem resolution strategies from youth fiction that illustrate in creative ways how imagination can be used to defuse bullying may prove particularly useful to youngsters.

- Ten long-term problem resolution strategies were identified and referenced. The common themes of personal empowerment, acceptance by the group, and the value of shared experiences for gaining empathy and understanding of the bully were noted.

- Designed primarily for the counseling staff's consideration, the process of bibliotherapy was developed and suggestions made for its effective use with both individuals and groups of students. Bibliotherapy refers to the use of books and stories in counseling and interpersonal-relationship training efforts.

- The narrative or restorying method refers to the use of fiction to initiate the process whereby young people come to retell their life stories with "happier" endings.

- Cross-cultural perspectives were found to be a significant resource for understanding conflict differently and responding accordingly.

CHAPTER 10

WHERE DO WE GO FROM HERE?

The Chapter One "Boxer" story is a slightly altered account of an incident that occurred in the sixth-grade class of this book's first author. Sara's circumstances did not improve, and ultimately she left the community. Could her story be rewritten with a more positive yet realistic denouement? We hope that anti-bullying methods set forth in this volume and the efforts of parents, students, and educators can change not only the average rates of bullying among students (as developed in Chapter Four) but the specific tales told by and about real students. In this spirit, we offer the following retelling of Sara's story.

Slightly overweight Sara was often the butt of Harold's jokes. Taking Harold's lead, many students called Sara "Boxer," after a popular cartoon character. While most of the abuse was verbal, students also poked and tripped Sara. Once, Harold even poured paint on one of Sara's books. A few of the boys made barking and howling noises when she walked into the room.

While several students actively bullied Sara and many conveniently ignored the situation, several recognized that Sara's treatment was unfair, and intervened on her behalf. Dan, one of the bigger boys, talked to Harold about the bullying, suggesting that Harold consider Sara's feelings. Of course, Harold teased Dan about protecting Sara. "Maybe you're in love with her," said the bully.

Though embarrassment made it difficult not to be hurt, Dan ignored Harold's mocking. He even made a point of speaking to Sara, telling her that most kids hated the bullying and promising that something would be done about it. These actions were extremely difficult for him as he feared for his own social status. He wouldn't have come to Sara's defense if the adults in his school and community had not consistently spoken out against bullying.

Anatol and Mary gently informed Harold that it "looked bad" for someone as big as he was to pick on a smaller person. Deborah pointed out that unwanted touching is sexual abuse, a very serious matter; Harold should "cut it the hell out." When exasperated, Deborah spoke out very directly.

Despite remonstrations from his peers, Harold continued to harass Sara. However, as students began to complain about his behavior, Harold seemed to have less and less influence—even over his cronies. Harold continued to pick on Sara, so Dan, Deborah, and Anatol spoke to Mr. Hazler, their homeroom teacher, who always seemed to have a sensitive ear for students' predicaments. Mr. Hazler expressed pride that the students had taken action against scapegoating and suggested that together they should enlist the help of Ms. Garrity, the school counselor.

Ms. Garrity was the person designated by the school discipline committee to deal with the most persistent and serious problems, such as bullying. After affirming that the incidents were taking place, Ms. Garrity met individually with Harold and Sara.

With Sara, Ms. Garrity supported the grieving process and affirmed that the bullying was a problem. They talked about Sara's feelings regarding her victimization and possible strategies for avoiding conflict while a more permanent resolution was sought.

The principal, Ms. Thomson, sent a letter to Harold's parents informing them that he had been picking on other students and that this would not be tolerated (in line with the school's published disciplinary standards). If any more incidents were verified, Harold would be isolated during recess for a short time. This was considered a natural consequence because the most troubling of his actions took place in situations where adult presence was minimal.

Meanwhile, Ms. Garrity interviewed Harold with an eye toward helping him to understand both the implications of bullying for Sara and her feelings. Considerable effort on Ms. Garrity's part was required over several sessions because Harold experienced difficulty empathizing with others. He believed that no one liked him and that he had to put on a tough front to keep from getting put down. He was not clear about specifically why he had picked on Sara. Finally, however, Harold verbalized remorse over the way Sara was treated and agreed to work out a plan. Harold and Sara even met together with Ms. Garrity to work up a plan about how they would interact.

Ms. Abernathy arranged time to work with Harold on his problem of thinking that everyone hated him. In addition, it turned out that he received rather harsh discipline at home and that his relationships with students echoed those with his father. At the request of the school social worker, Harold's parents agreed to seek family counseling and were referred to an appropriate agency.

Sara's life was not perfect; she was bothered by feelings of inadequacy about her appearance resulting from the bullying she had received. She found it difficult to trust other students, even though she knew objectively that they had "gone to bat for her." Sara slowly began to enjoy school again as she was taught by her counselor to assert herself in situations where she had formerly acted passively. In addition, she learned to make more positive self-statements to counteract situations where her ego was threatened.

The above scene may appear unrealistic. Is it not a pie-in-the-sky hope that young people, not to mention adults, would react so effectively to bullying? As an institution, the school described above seems too good to be true. Or is it? Certainly, as things currently stand, the above story is hard to believe. We probably fail to see humane possibilities because we are used to a world where students do not feel obligated to help one another. The most significant failing of adults vis-à-vis children in contemporary society may be a lack of vision regarding violence-free schools.

Due in part to our lack of imagination, many students cannot envision schools or a society where they are free from harassment. For example, many youngsters do not recognize violence on television when they see it because they are inured to it. Filmmakers require ever larger splashes of blood before audiences will be titillated out of their hard-earned cash. As a result of the sea of violence through which they swim, many young people don't even notice verbal aggression. We must help them learn again to see what is happening when one person or group oppresses others—even with words.

We fear that the late twentieth century is a time when increasingly individuals are seen as islands, and care for the less unfortunate is portrayed in some circles as a burden on "productive" members of society. Based on our discussions with students, we believe that this alienation places a hard and angry edge on human relationships in schools and other social institutions. The principle that is most inclusive of the anti-bullying ideas presented in these pages is the notion of community. Schools must become cohesive, integrated, family-like villages in which each student has a place, and a sense of mutuality and regard is inculcated along with literacy and numeracy. Until this occurs, all efforts to reduce violence, including bullying, will be, at best, stop-gap measures.

Summary

- It is difficult for us to imagine a school where students would refrain from picking on others, where bystanders would intervene, and where students possessed the skills to deal with bullying effectively. Our inability to imagine such a school is part of the problem.

- Developing a sense of community is a central theme that holds together all anti-bullying efforts.

EPILOGUE

The material that could be addressed in a book on bullying is nearly endless, because so many of our social concerns center on the treatment of the weak by the strong. For example, the interface between racial hatred and bullying probably deserves a chapter of its own. We feel that we have merely touched on the issues of sexism and prejudice based on appearance in these pages—topics with their own paradigms and research methods. Decisions about what to include in this book were difficult.

Nonetheless, several topics not previously mentioned deserve the attention of practitioners as they design programs to reduce bullying. A brief mention is made in these end notes of aspects of bullying and related phenomena that found no natural "site" in the pages of this book. Several evaluation and research issues deserve special attention in the future. Legal concerns related to bullying deserve mention, as does the role of moral, spiritual, and communitarian ideals in reducing child-on-child aggression.

Evaluation and Research Issues

Delivering information to teachers was deemed crucial to the success of bullying reduction programs. Researchers and practitioners must develop defensible methods for tracking the responses of educators and other helping professionals to bullying and efforts to reduce the problem.

A critical effort will be to trace the effects of bullying reduction programs on later rates of violent crime. It is reasonable to expect that, as was the case in Norway, effective anti-bullying campaigns will produce positive effects on related behaviors—but this is not yet established.

Legal Concerns

Many bullying behaviors are not just wrong—they are illegal. Some situations are too serious for treatment via teaching and counseling alone. Persistent sexual harassment, for example, fits this category. Educators are bound by Title IX of the 1972 Education Act and Title VII of the 1964 Civil Rights Act (Marczely, 1993). The courts have ruled that persons in the workplace must not suffer hostile environments based on their gender. In addition, they have ruled that for legal purposes, schools are bound by the same rules (Shoop, 1994).

Schools are facing an increasing number of sexual harassment suits under Title IX. There is every reason to believe that such litigation will continue. Students have won monetary settlements when schools have failed to protect them from sexual harassment by other students. Clearly, effective anti-bullying efforts such as those outlined in these pages may be fundamental to a school's reasonable discharge of its legal responsibilities (Lawton, 1993).

Sexual harassment lawsuits are not the only legal aspect of bullying and its prevention. Recently, a case in North Dakota went all the way to the Supreme Court of that state (Lister, 1995). The family of a student served with a restraining order enjoining their son from bullying a younger student appealed their case on the grounds of the First Amendment right to free speech. The North Dakota Supreme Court, in a case receiving considerable national publicity, ruled against the plaintiff and in favor of the scapegoat, employing state anti-stalking statutes as the legal mechanism for enforcing the restraining order. It is only a short step from restraining orders to tort litigation against public schools that fail to take prudent measures to defend the rights of students to learn in peace.

Physical attacks can do more than hurt feelings—often, they fall into the category of assault and battery. Educators must be trained to recognize situations that require the aid of outside authorities.

Advocating for Youth

It may not be enough to teach and counsel. Increasing numbers of our young people are in distress from poverty and the ills of abuse and neglect. It is important that educators communicate their regard for young people by advocating for them in appropriate forums. Is it not a form of symbolic bullying that a quarter of the children in the United States live in poverty? Perhaps this reflects a society not entirely certain of its attitude toward children.

Moral, Ethical, and Spiritual Issues

In the end, bullying is related to our ultimate beliefs about the worth of individuals and the way they should be treated. The topics of morality, moral education, ethical reasoning, and spirituality lie at the core of society's problems, including child-on-child aggression.

As practitioners think about bullying in the future, it would be beneficial to examine the role that moral development plays in learning to care about one another. Educational leaders may look to the world's religions for answers to the problems of how we interrelate. For example, the Judeo-Christian-Islamic view that man is created in the image of God has enormous moral implications for how the weakest among us are treated. In the Christian tradition, Jesus stated that whatever was done to the weakest was done to him. This is another example of a moral teaching that can be brought to bear on the problem of bullying. Protection of the weak and respect for the individual transcend nearly all religions and ethical codes and may also be brought to bear on the issue of bullying.

We hope that these ending issues round out the picture of bullying and that interested readers will be motivated to study, research, and most of all, take action. Plenty of work remains for everyone.

Summary

- In evaluating bullying prevention programs, the views of teachers must be assessed.

- The present climate of litigiousness makes it important for school officials to do all they can to safeguard students. Male-on-female bullying is actionable under Title IX of the Education Amendments.

- Helping professionals should consider political and social advocacy for youth as a professional responsibility. Bullying is probably exacerbated by social problems facing young people.

- Moral, ethical, and religious principles have a role to play in preventing bullying. This aspect must be explored in more depth during the coming years.

REFERENCES

Adler, C.S. (1982). *The once in a while hero.* New York: Coward, McCann, & Geoghegan.

Alberti, R.E., & Emmons, M.L. (1982). *Your perfect right: A guide to assertive behavior,* 4th ed. San Luis, Obispo, CA: Impact.

Alberto, P.A., & Troutman, A.C. (1995). *Applied behavior analysis for teachers,* 4th ed. Englewood Cliffs, NJ: Merrill.

Amatea, J., & Fabrick, F. (1984). Moving a family into therapy: Critical referral issues for the school counselor. *The School Counselor, 31,* 285–294.

American Association of University Women and Lewis Harris Associates (1993). Hostile hallways: The AAUW survey on sexual harassment in America's schools. Annapolis Junction, MD: Author (Eric Document Reproduction Service No. ED 356 186).

Anderson, C.S. (1982). The search for school climate: A review of the research. *Review of Educational Research, 52,* 368–420.

Arora, C.M., & Thompson, D.A. (1987). Defining bullying for a secondary school. *Educational and Child Psychology, 4,* 110–120.

Auruch, K., Black, P.W., & Scimicca, J.A. (1991). *Conflict resolution: Cross cultural perspectives.* New York: Greenwood Press.

Bandura, A., & Walters, R.H. (1963). *Social learning and personality development.* New York: Holt, Rinehart, & Winston.

Beavers, W.R. (1985). *Successful marriage: A family systems approach to couples therapy.* New York: W. W. Norton & Company.

Becvar, D.S., & Becvar, R.J. (1988). *Family therapy: A systemic integration.* Boston: Allyn & Bacon.

Bellack, A.S., & Hersen, M. (1977). *Behavior modification: An introductory textbook.* Baltimore: Williams & Wilkins.

Bertalanffy, L. (1968). *General systems theory.* New York: George Braziller.

Beuchert, M.E., Goodman, A.J.S., and Long, N.J. (Eds.) (1990). *Walking through the storm: Working with aggressive children and youth.* Silver Spring, MD: NAK Production Associates and Starr Commonwealth School. (Features two videotapes and instructional guide.)

Bolton, F.G., & Bolton, S.R. (1987). *Working with violent families: A guide for clinical and legal practitioners.* Newbury Park, CA: Sage Publications.

Brooks, J. (1980). *Make me a hero.* New York: Dutton.

Bryant, A.L. (1993). Hostile hallways: The AAUW survey on sexual harassment in America's schools. *Journal of School Health, 63,* 355–358.

Carrick, C. (1982). *What a wimp.* New York: Clarion Books.

Chazan, M. (1989). Bullying in the infant school. In D.P. Tattum & D.A. Lane (Eds.), *Bullying in schools* (pp. 33–43). Stoke-on-Trent, England: Trentham Books.

Coleman, J.C. (1980). Friendship and the peer group in adolescence. In J. Adelson (Ed.), *Handbook of adolescent psychology.* New York: Wiley.

Conford, E. (1980). *The revenge of the incredible Dr. Rancid and his youthful assistant, Jeffrey.* Boston: Little, Brown.

Constantine, L. (1978). Family sculpture and relationship mapping techniques. *Journal of Marriage and Family Counseling, 4*(2), 13–23.

Cook, A.S., & Dworkin, D.S. (1992). *Helping the bereaved: Therapeutic interventions for children, adolescents, and adults.* New York: Basic Books.

Corey, G. (1991). *Theory and practice of counseling and psychotherapy,* 4th ed. Pacific Grove, CA: Brooks/Cole Publishing Company.

Crum, T.F. (1987). *Magic of conflict.* New York: Simon & Schuster.

Duhl, B.S. (1983). *From the inside out and other metaphors: Creative and integrative approaches to training in systems thinking.* New York: Brunner/Mazel.

Dreikurs, R. (1953). *Fundamentals of Adlerian psychology.* Chicago: Alfred Adler Institute.

_____ (1968). *Psychology in the classroom,* 2d ed. New York: Harper & Row.

Eggert, L.L. (1994). *Anger management for youth: Stemming aggression and violence.* Bloomington, IN: National Educational Service.

Ehly, S.W., & Larson, S.C. (1980). *Peer tutoring for individualized instruction.* Boston: Allyn & Bacon.

Eron, L.D. (1987). Aggression through the ages. *School Safety,* Fall, 12–16.

Fenell, D.L., & Weinhold, B.K. (1989). *Counseling families: An introduction to marital and family therapy.* Denver: Love Publishing Company.

Floyd, N.M. (1985). 'Pick on someone your own size': Controlling victimization. *Pointer, 29*(2), 9–17.

References

Garrity, C., Jens, K., Porter, W., Sager, N., & Short-Camilli, C. (1995). *Bully proofing your school: A comprehensive approach for elementary schools.* Longmont, CO: Sopris West.

Gilmartin, B.G. (1987). Peer group antecedents of severe love shyness in males. *Journal of Personality, 55,* 467–489.

Golden, L.B. (1983). Brief family interventions in a school setting. *Elementary School Guidance and Counseling,17,* 288–293.

_____ (1988). Quick assessment for family functioning. *The School Counselor, 35,* 179–184.

Goldstein, A.P., Sprafkin, R.P., Gershaw, N.J., & Klein, P. (1980). *Skillstreaming the adolescent: A structured learning approach to teaching prosocial skills.* Champaign, IL: Research Press.

Greenbaum, S., Turner, B., & Stephens, R.D. (1989). *Set straight on bullies.* Malibu, CA: Pepperdine University Press.

Griffiths, H. (1983). *Rafa's dog.* New York: Holiday House.

Gurman, A.S., & Kniskern, D.P. (1981). *Handbook of family therapy, vol. 1.* New York: Brunner/Mazel.

_____ (1991). *Handbook of family therapy, vol. 2.* New York: Brunner/Mazel.

Hall, R.V., & Hall, M.C. (1982). *How to negotiate a behavioral contract.* Austin, TX: Pro Ed.

Hartman, A., & Laird, J. (1983). *Family-centered social work practice.* New York: The Free Press.

Hazler, R.J., Hoover, J.H., & Oliver, R. (1991). Student perceptions of victimization by bullies in school. *Journal of Humanistic Education and Development, 29,* 143–150.

_____ (1992). What kids say about bullying. *The Executive Educator, 4*(11), 20–22.

Hetrick, E.S., & Martin, A.D. (1987). *Developmental issues and their resolution for gay and lesbian adolescents.* New York: Haworth Press.

Hoover, J.H. (in press). *The prevention of schoolyard bullying.* York, PA: The William Gladden Foundation.

Hoover, J.H., & Hazler, R J. (1991). Bullies and victims. *Elementary School Guidance and Counseling, 25,* 212–219.

Hoover, J.H., & Juul, K. (1993). Bullying in Europe and the U.S. *The Journal of Emotional and Behavioral Problems, 1*(2), 25–29.

Hoover, J.H., Oliver, R.L., & Hazler, R.J. (1992). Bullying: Perceptions of adolescent victims in the Midwestern USA. *School Psychology International, 13*(1), 5–16.

Hoover, J.H., Oliver, R.L., & Thomson, K.A. (1993). Perceived victimization by school bullies: New research and future direction. *Journal of Humanistic Education and Development, 32,* 76–84.

Hopper, N.J. (1984). *Hang on, Harvey!* New York: Dell.

Ivey, A. (1988). *Intentional interviewing and counseling,* 2d ed. Pacific Grove, CA: Brooks/Cole Publishing Company.

Johnson, D.W., & Johnson, R.T. (1994). *Learning together and alone: Cooperative, competitive, and individualistic learning,* 4th ed. Boston: Allyn & Bacon.

Knowlton, D.D., & Muhlhauser, T.L. (1994). Mediation in the presence of domestic violence: Is it the light at the end of the tunnel or is a train on the track? *North Dakota Law Review, 70,* 255–268.

Kottman, T., & Stiles, K. (1990). Mutual storytelling: An intervention for depressed and suicidal children. *The School Counselor, 37,* 337–342.

Kreidler, W.J. (1984). *Creative conflict resolution: More than 200 activities for keeping peace in the classroom, K-6.* New York: Scott, Foresman & Company.

Kropp, P. (1980). *Wilted.* New York: Coward, McCann, & Geoghegan.

Lawton, M. (1993). Sexual harassment of students the target of district policies. *Education Week, 12*(20), 15–16.

Lee, J. (1993). *Facing the fire: Experiencing and expressing anger appropriately.* New York: Bantam Books.

Lister, P. (1995). Bullies: The big new problem you must know about. *Redbook,* November, pp. 116–119, 136, 138.

Long, N.J. (1995). Why adults strike back: Learned behavior or genetic code? *Reclaiming Children and Youth: Journal of Emotional and Behavioral Problems, 4*(1), 11–15.

Marczely, B. (1993). A legal update on sexual harassment in the public schools. *The Clearing House, 66*(6), 329–331.

Mauser, P.R. (1982). *A bundle of sticks.* New York: Atheneum.

Maxwell, J. (1989). Mediation in schools: Self regulation, self esteem, and self discipline. *Mediation Quarterly,* Winter, 149–155.

McMullin, R.E. (1986). *Handbook of cognitive therapy techniques.* New York: Norton.

Meichenbaum, D. (1977). *Cognitive behavior modification: An integrative approach.* New York: Plenum.

_____ (1985). *Stress inoculation training.* New York: Pergamon Press.

_____ (1986). Cognitive behavior modification. In F.H. Kanfer & A.P. Goldstein (Eds.), *Helping people change: A textbook of methods* (pp. 346–380). New York: Pergamon Press.

Mihashi, O. (1987). The symbolism of social discrimination: A decoding of discriminatory language. *Current Anthropology, 28,* 519–520.

Minuchin, S. (1974). *Families and family therapy.* Cambridge, MA: Harvard University Press.

Mosak, H. (1989). Adlerian psychotherapy. In R.J. Corsini & D. Wedding (Eds.), *Current psychotherapies,* 4th ed. (pp. 65–116). Itasca, IL: F. E. Peacock.

Munthe, E. (1989). Bullying in Scandinavia. In D.A. Lane (Ed.), *Bullying: An international perspective* (pp. 66–78). London: Professional Development Foundation.

References

Nichols, M.P., & Schwartz, R.C. (1991). *Family therapy concepts and methods,* 2d ed. Boston: Allyn & Bacon.

Ohlsson, I. (1992). Hur fungerar integreringen as sarskolelever i grundskolen? [How effective is the integration of mentally retarded pupils in the elementary school?] *Nordisk Tiddskrift fur Spesialpedagogikk, 2,* 14–15.

Oliver, R.O., Hoover, J.H., & Hazler, R.J. (1994). The perceived roles of bullying in small-town midwestern schools. *Journal of Counseling and Development, 72,* 416–420.

Oliver, R., Oaks, I.N., & Hoover, J.H. (1993). Family issues and interventions in bully/victim relationships. *The School Counselor,* 41, 129–202.

Oliver, R.L., Young, T.A., & LaSalle, S.M. (1994). Bullying and victimization: The help and hindrance of children's literature. *The School Counselor, 42,* 137–146.

Olson, D.H., Russell, C.S., & Sprenkle, D.H. (1983). Circumplex model of marital and family systems. *Family Process,* 22, 69–84.

Olweus, D. (1978). *Aggression in the schools: Bullies and whipping boys.* Washington, DC: Hemisphere.

_____ (1980). Familial and temperamental determinants of aggressive behaviors in adolescent boys: A causal analysis. *Developmental Psychology, 16,* 644–660.

_____ (1984). Aggressors and their victims: Bullying in school. In N. Frude and H. Gault (Eds.), *Disruptive behavior in schools.* New York: Wiley.

_____ (1991). Bully/victim problems among schoolchildren: Basic facts and effects of a school based intervention program. In D.J. Pepler & K.H. Rubin (Eds.), *The development and treatment of childhood aggression* (pp. 411–448). Hillsdale, NJ: Lawrence Erlbaum.

_____ (1992). Victimization by peers: Antecedents and long-term outcomes. In K.H. Rubin and J.B. Asendorf (Eds.), *Social withdrawal, inhibition, and shyness in childhood.* London: Erlbaum.

Olweus, D., & Alsaker, F. (1991). Assessing change in a cohort-longitudinal study with hierarchical data. In D. Magnusson, L.R. Bergman, G. Rudinger, & B. Torestad (Eds.), *Problems and methods in longitudinal research: Stability and change* (pp. 107–132). Cambridge: Cambridge University Press.

O'Moore, A.M. (1989). Bullying in Britain and Ireland: An overview. In E. Munthe & E. Roland (Eds.), *Bullying: An international perspective* (pp. 2–21). London: David Fulton, Publishers.

Patterson, G.R. (1982). *Coercive family process.* Eugene, OR: Castalia.

Patterson, G.R., DeBaryshe, B.D., & Ramsey, E. (1989). A developmental perspective on antisocial behavior. *American Psychologist, 44,* 329–335.

Pawluck, C.J. (1989). Social construction of teasing. *Journal for the Theory of Social Behavior, 19,* 145–167.

Perry, D.G., Kusel, S.J., & Perry, L.C. (1988). Victims of peer aggression. *Developmental Psychology, 24,* 807–814.

Perske, R., & Perske, M. (1988). *Circles of friends.* Nashville, TN: Abingdon Press.

Piercy, F.P., & Sprenkle, D.H. (1986). *Family therapy sourcebook*. New York: The Guilford Press.

Pikas, A. (1989a). A pure concept of mobbing gives the best results for treatment. *School Psychology International, 10*, 95–104.

_____ (1989b). The common concern method for the treatment of mobbing. In David A. Lane (Ed.), *Bullying: An international perspective*. London: David Fulton, Publishers.

Pipher, M. (1994). *Reviving Ophelia. Saving the selves of adolescent girls*. New York: Ballantine Books.

Prothrow-Stith, D. (1994). A public health model builds nonviolence into the curriculum. *Educational Digest, 6*(3), 30–34.

Remboldt, Carole (1994). *Solving violence in your school: Why a systematic approach is necessary*. Minneapolis, MN: Johnson Institute-QVS, Inc.

_____ (1994). *Violence in schools: The enabling factor*. Minneapolis, MN: Johnson Institute-QVS. Inc.

Robins, L.N. (1966). *Deviant children grow up*. Baltimore: Williams and Wilkins.

Roland, E. (1989). A system oriented strategy against bullying. In David A. Lane (Ed.), *Bullying: An international perspective* (pp. 143–151). London: David Fulton, Publishers.

Rubin, R.A., & Balow, B. (1978). Prevalence of teacher-identified behavior problems: A longitudinal study. *Exceptional Children, 45*, 102–111.

Sachar, L. (1989). *The boy who lost his face*. New York: Trumpet Club.

Samovar, L.L, & Porter, R.E. (Eds.) (1991). *Intercultural communication: A reader,* 6th ed. Belmont, CA: Wadsworth Publishing.

Scribner, V. (1993). *Gopher takes heart*. New York: Viking.

Shakeshaft, C., Barber, E., Hergenrother, Johnson, Y.M., Mandel, L.S., & Sawyer, J. (1995). Peer harassment in schools. *Journal for a Just and Caring Education, 1*, 30–44.

Sherer, M.L. (1993). No longer just child's play: School liability under Title IX for peer sexual harassment. *University of Pennsylvania Law Review, 141*, 2119–2168.

Shoop, J.G. (1994). Beyond horseplay: Students sue schools over sexual harassment. *Trial, 30*(6), 12–14.

Siskind, L. (1992). *The hopscotch tree*. New York: Bantam, Doubleday, Dell Books.

Smith, P.K. (1991). The silent nightmare: bullying and victimization in school peer groups. *The Psychologist: Bulletin of the British Psychological Society, 4*, 243–248.

Stephenson, P., & Smith, D. (1989). Bullying in the junior school. In D.P. Tattum and D.A. Lane (Eds.), *Bullying in school* (pp. 45–57). Stoke-on-Trent, England: Trentham Books.

Thomas, J.R. (1984). *Courage at Indian Deep*. New York: Clarion Books.

Thomas, M.B. (1992). *An introduction to marital and family therapy*. New York: Macmillan.

References

Walker, H.M. (1993). Anti-social behavior in school. *Journal of Emotional and Behavioral Problems, 2*(1), 20–24.

Walker, H.M., Colvin, G., & Ramsey, E. (1995). *Antisocial behaviors in school: Strategies and best practices.* Pacific Grove, CA: Brooks/Cole.

Webster-Doyle, T. (1991). *Why is everybody always picking on me? A guide to understanding bullies.* Middlebury, CT: Atrium Society.

White, M., & Epston, D. (1990). *Narrative means to therapeutic ends.* New York: Norton.

Wilcoxin, S.A., & Comas, R.E. (1987). Contemporary trends in family counseling: What do they mean for the school counselor? *The School Counselor, 34,* 219–225.

Wolpe, J. (1990). *The practice of behavior therapy,* 4th ed. New York: Pergamon.

APPENDICES

E

EVALUATION TOOLS

National Educational Service

BULLYING SURVEY: FORM B

Instructions: Please help make your school a better place to live, grow, and learn by answering some questions about the way people act toward one another in the school. Your answers will help your teachers, principals, and counselors learn more about the way this school "feels" to you and your friends. There are no right or wrong answers to any of the questions. We want to know what you really think about the way things are at your school.

Your answers will be kept strictly confidential. This means that no one will know your name, the name of any of your classmates, or of your teachers. Again, the idea of the survey is to learn how you see your school so that adults in the building, together with you, can design a more student-friendly school!

> Bullying definition: We want to know what *you* think about bullying, but you can start by thinking of bullying as one or a group of students picking on another student or treating them in a way that they do not like.

A. ABOUT YOU

Sex (circle one): FEMALE   MALE   Age (years) _____ Grade _____

B. BULLYING AT SCHOOL

Please answer the questions as directed.

1. Have you ever been bullied by other students (during any school year)? Circle your answer below (circle only one).

       YES   NO

2. During which school year were you most troubled by bullying? Write a grade in the blank space.

    Worst grade for bullying: _____ (It does not have to be at this school.)

Please use the following scale when you answer the next group of questions about bullying (Numbers 3–10).

> 0 = **has not happened this past month**
> 1–2 = **has happened 1 or 2 times this past month**
> 3–4 = **has happened 3 or 4 times this past month**
> more = **has happened more often than 4 times this past month**

Remember, circle 1, 2, 3, or 4, depending on how often these things have happened over the past month. All of the items and questions refer to what happens to you at school or on the way to and from school.

3. How often have you been bullied at school **over the past month**?

    How often this month? (circle only one):   0   1–2   3–4   more

4. How often have you been physically attacked, **over the past month** (at school)? That is, how often have you been hit, kicked, punched, pinched, tripped, or something like these?

    How often this month? (circle only one):   0   1–2   3–4   more

5. How often have you been touched by someone in a way you did not like **over the past month** (at school or on the way to and from school)?

    How often this month? (circle only one):   0   1–2   3–4   more

6. How often have you been teased over the past month (at school)?

    How often this month? (circle only one):   0   1–2   3–4   more

7. How often during **the past month** has someone said something cruel to you either at school or on the way to and from school?

    How often this month? (circle only one):   0   1–2   3–4   more

8. During the past month, how often has someone excluded you on purpose? That is, how often has someone kept you out of things you'd like to do?

    How often this month? (circle only one):   0   1–2   3–4   more

9. How often over the past month has someone played a practical joke on you?

    How often this month? (circle only one):   0   1–2   3–4   more

10. How often over the past month has someone left you out of activities or refused to play or socialize with you?

    How often this month? (circle only one):   0   1–2   3–4   more

C. WHO DOES THE BULLYING?

1. Over the past month, the bullying I received was from (check only one box):

No one, I was not bullied.	I was bullied mostly by **boys**.	I was bullied mostly by **girls**.	I was bullied by **both boys and girls**.

2. The age of kids who bullied me was (check only one box):

No one, I was not bullied.	Only kids younger than me.	Only kids my own age/grade.	Both younger and older kids.

3. If you were bullied, how well did school officials handle it? (Check only one box.)

I was not bullied over the past month.	Adults at school did not deal with the bullying at all.	Adults at school handled the bullying poorly.	Adults at school handled the bullying well.

4. How well do school officials handle the bullying of others you have seen at your school? (Check only one box.)

I never saw anyone bullied.	Adults at school did not deal with the bullying at all.	Adults at school handled the bullying poorly.	Adults at school handled the bullying well.

5. Overall, how would you rate the efforts of adults at your school to prevent students from picking on one another? (Check only one box.)

Very good	Good	Poor	Very Poor

6. Overall, how would you rate the efforts of adults (teachers/principal) to make your school a safe place in which to learn? (Check only one box.)

Very good	Good	Poor	Very Poor

D. WHERE DOES THE BULLYING OCCUR?

Put an X in each box that describes a place at school, or coming to and from school, where you have been bullied this past month (if any). Check all that are true for you.

1. On the school bus . . . . ❑
2. Playground . . . . ❑
3. Walking to or from school . . . . ❑
4. Classroom . . . . ❑
5. Lunch room . . . . ❑
6. Hallways . . . . ❑
7. Gym . . . . ❑
8. Locker room . . . . ❑
9. Other (you write in *places* where you've been picked on)

_____

_____

_____

E. ATTITUDES ABOUT BULLYING

Please show how much you agree or disagree with the following statements:

1. Most teasing I see is done in fun, not to hurt people.

    How much do you agree? (circle one)

    agree very much   agree   disagree   disagree very much

2. Most students who get bullied bring it on themselves.

    How much do you agree? (circle one)

    agree very much   agree   disagree   disagree very much

3. Bullying helps people by teaching them what is important to the group.

    How much do you agree? (circle one)

    agree very much   agree   disagree   disagree very much

4. Bullying helps people by making them tougher.

    How much do you agree? (circle one)

    agree very much   agree   disagree   disagree very much

PLEASE WRITE ANYTHING YOU'D LIKE TO ADD ABOUT BULLYING AT YOUR SCHOOL BELOW.

THANK YOU FOR COMPLETING THE SURVEY.

BULLYING SURVEY: FORM P

Instructions. Please help us make our school a better place to live, grow, and learn by answering questions about the way you learn and about the way that people act toward one another at school. Your answers will help your principal, teachers, and counselors learn more about how you feel about school and how to make it a good place to grow and learn.

Your answers will be kept strictly confidential. This means that no one will know your name, the name of your school, the name of any of your classmates, or of your teachers. Again, the survey is to learn how you see your school so that adults in the building, in partnership with you, can design a more student-friendly school!

> Bullying definition: We want to know what *you* think about bullying, but you can start by thinking of bullying as one or a group of students picking on another student or treating them in a way that they do not like.

Below you will find two sets of questions. One set of questions deals with the amount of time your teachers have spent on certain activities over the past month. The second set of questions asks you to rate how worthwhile the activities were. **There are no right or wrong answers!**

PART A. ABOUT YOU

Sex (circle one): FEMALE   MALE   Age (years) _____ Grade _____

PART B. ACTIVITIES

Please use the following scale to rate the amount of time any teacher or other adult at school (principal or counselor) has spent performing the described activities over the past month.

> **0 = no adult at school did this**
> **1 = one class period was spent on this activity**
> **2–5 = two to five class periods were spent on this activity**
> **more = more than five class periods were spent on this activity**

1. Working on activities related to how people get along with one another

    How many class periods? (circle only one):   0   1   2–5   more

2. Talking about bullying or students picking on one another

    How many class periods? (circle only one):   0   1   2–5   more

Please turn to the next page and continue the survey.

3. Reprimanding students for misbehavior toward one another

How many class periods? (circle only one):   0   1   2–5   more

4. Discussing interpersonal relationships or social relationships (talking about how people get along with each other)

How many class periods? (circle only one):   0   1   2–5   more

5. Talking about how the different races get along at school

How many class periods? (circle only one):   0   1   2–5   more

6. Working on how males and females (boys & girls) get along together in the school

How many class periods? (circle only one):   0   1   2–5   more

7. Discussing teasing, mocking, or making fun

How many class periods? (circle only one):   0   1   2–5   more

Quality of school activities. Use the following scale to rate how useful the following activities were to **you**, in your personal life, as you learn to get along with others. Mark "**0**" if the listed activity was **not done** in school **over the past month**.

0 = the activity was not done
1 = the activity was done but was not helpful to you
2 = the activity was helpful to you

1. Activities related to learning about how students get along

How useful? (circle only one):   0   1   2

2. Class talks about bullying or why students pick on one another

How useful? (circle only one):   0   1   2

3. Talks about, or activities related to, teasing or mocking

How useful? (circle only one):   0   1   2

4. Discussions of how males and females get along in the school

How useful? (circle only one):   0   1   2

5. Talks about how races get along in the school

How useful? (circle only one):   0   1   2

Please turn to the next page and continue the survey.

C. More Information

1. Would you like to learn more about how to get along with other students?

    (circle one)   YES   NO

2. Do adults at this school (teachers, parents, counselors) work with you on how to get along with others?

    (circle one)   YES   NO

3. I believe there is a problem with bullies at this school.

    (circle one)   YES   NO

4. If you think there is a problem with bullies, do you believe the adults in your school are doing **something** about it?

    (circle one)   NO BULLY PROBLEM   YES   NO

5. If you think there is a bully problem at your school, do you believe that adults are doing **enough** about it?

    (circle one)   NO BULLY PROBLEM   YES   NO

Write any comments below about how well adults at your school work on bullying problems and/or write what could be done about these problems.

Thank you for filling out the survey.

SUGGESTED INTERVIEW QUESTIONS

Note: It is recommended that these questions be used as a starting point for a qualitative evaluation of the bullying intervention program. Note that it may be useful to employ individuals who have had some training in interviewing or in qualitative research methods.

These questions could be posed to a random sample of students or could be addressed to a panel via focus-group-type methodology. However used, it is important that directions to individual or groups of students emphasize the confidential nature of responses. In addition, it is extremely central that student responses during these exercises be accepted with equanimity by interviewers if data are to reflect the life of the school with some veracity. Audiotaping is recommended; it is important to ask students' permission to record information: always stress confidentiality.

1. What is it like here at _____[name of school]? That is, what is the feeling or climate like here? Describe it.

2. Generally speaking, how well do students get along with one another?

3. Are there identifiable [nameable] groups? What are the names of the main groups?

4. Is it common that certain students hang together? If so, could these groups be described with names? How do members of the groups relate to one another? For example, how do the [athletes] get along with [artsy] students?

5. Tell me some things that teachers or other adults in the building do to make student relationships better?

6. What are some things that teachers or other adults do that make things worse between students?

7. In your view, what is bullying?

8. What are some behaviors that make up bullying? [What might student A do to pick on student B?]

9. How much bullying [picking on/scapegoating] goes on at _____ [name of school]?

10. How does bullying affect young people? Can you provide an example?

11. Is it important to reduce bullying here?

12. If so, why? If not, why not?

13. Have adults [teachers, counselors, administrators] in the building done anything to reduce bullying?

14. If yes to #13, what?

15. If yes to #13, how has it been going?

16. Specifically, what has worked? What hasn't? Why?

17. Do some students get picked on more often than others? If so, why?

18. Why do other students get picked on?

19. Do you get picked on frequently? If so, why?

20. How do you or others handle bullying?

21. How do you feel when you see someone being picked on?

22. Do you ever step in when someone is being bullied? Why or why not?

23. What causes some students to become bullies?

24. How do you feel about bullying? Is there anything you'd like adults in the building to know about it?

25. What have you learned from any discussions of bullying?

26. Generally, how does this school *feel* to you?

STUDENT EVALUATION OF COUNSELING SERVICES

Instructions. Please help us make our school's counseling services the best that they can be by answering these questions.

For each of the statements given below, circle the answer that best describes your thoughts and feelings about the counseling help you received at school for the problem of bullying or being bullied by others.

1. The Counselor really listened to me and understood my problem(s).

   How much do you agree? (circle one)

   agree very much   agree   disagree   disagree very much

2. The Counselor gave me enough time to talk things out and better understand the problem(s) I was facing.

   How much do you agree? (circle one)

   agree very much   agree   disagree   disagree very much

3. The Counselor helped me to solve my problem(s) with bullying or being bullied.

   How much do you agree? (circle one)

   agree very much   agree   disagree   disagree very much

4. I believe that the counseling I received helped me to feel safer while at school.

   How much do you agree? (circle one)

   agree very much   agree   disagree   disagree very much

5. The Counselor treated me with kindness and respect.

   How much do you agree? (circle one)

   agree very much   agree   disagree   disagree very much

6. The Counselor did not put me down or make fun of me.

   How much do you agree? (circle one)

   agree very much   agree   disagree   disagree very much

7. The Counselor encouraged me while I was trying to solve my problem(s).

   How much do you agree? (circle one)

   agree very much   agree   disagree   disagree very much

8. When talking with me, the Counselor used words that I knew and could understand easily.

    How much do you agree? (circle one)

    agree very much   agree   disagree   disagree very much

9. I felt like the Counselor really cared about me and my problem(s).

    How much do you agree? (circle one)

    agree very much   agree   disagree   disagree very much

10. The Counselor gave me a chance to learn better how other students feel about me and how I feel about others.

    How much do you agree? (circle one)

    agree very much   agree   disagree   disagree very much

11. Counseling helped me to learn what I needed to know about how to treat others and act better at school.

    How much do you agree? (circle one)

    agree very much   agree   disagree   disagree very much

12. Counseling helped me to better know my strengths and to understand what I do well.

    How much do you agree? (circle one)

    agree very much   agree   disagree   disagree very much

13. I am very happy with the help that I got from my Counselor.

    How much do you agree? (circle one)

    agree very much   agree   disagree   disagree very much

Instructions: For the next three questions, simply print the answers in your own words that most honestly answer the questions.

14. What I liked best about counseling was _____

    _____

    _____

15. What I liked least about counseling was _____

    _____

    _____

16. How many times did you visit with the Counselor about your problem with bullying or being bullied by others? _____

APPENDICES

R | ROLE PLAY SCENARIOS

National Educational Service

Role Play Scenarios for Use in Classrooms

Pick on Someone Your Own Size

Scene

Sixth-graders Barb and Sam are walking and chatting together in the halls. It is after school, so not many other people are around. Sam is a smaller-than-average student. Robert, a big, athletic youngster, walks up to Sam and begins teasing him for being a wimp. Robert teases Sam for being in the math club rather than on the football team. Barb also receives some teasing for walking with Sam.

Questions and Tasks

1. Describe the feelings of each person in the scenario.

2. What are some reasons that Robert may have picked on Sam?

3. Is the situation, as played, an example of bullying? Why or why not?

Less than Stylish

Scene

A group of four girls, including Ella and Samantha, are standing in a circle waiting to go into home room. Ella, a seemingly confident eighth-grader, is pretty and has many friends. She teases Samantha gently about Sam's less-than-stylish clothes. Samantha takes the teasing for a while but gets angrier and angrier. She has never liked to talk about her clothes. Samantha uses this episode to stop the teasing.

Questions and Tasks

1. What happened during the scene?

2. How did Samantha attempt to get the teasing to stop?

3. Suggest some alternative things she could have done.

Will Eileen go to the Movies?

Scene

Bob, an eighth-grade boy, really likes Eileen. In the scene, he is asking her for a date as they walk across the schoolgrounds on their way home after school. He wants to take her to a movie and out for a sandwich. Eileen does not want to go at all. Bob, however, does not like to be turned down and can sometimes be very persistent.

QUESTIONS AND TASKS

1. What do you think Bob was thinking at the beginning of the scenario?

2. Did Bob's attitude or behavior change as the exchange continued?

3. What is the problem Eileen is faced with?

4. Describe how she handled it. Did she make herself clear?

WHAT A DUMMY

SCENE

Roberto works very hard in his eighth-grade science class. Because of his reading problems, however, he has a hard time keeping up. Usually, Roberto is a cheerful person with a great sense of humor. Today, however, he erupts in anger when Sally calls him a dummy. She does this quietly, but she is frustrated because she feels that Roberto is slowing down the science class—her favorite. The scene takes place in the hall just after science class, and at least two bystanders hear the remark and stop to listen to the argument.

QUESTIONS AND TASKS

1. Do you think that the bystanders affected Roberto's mood?

2. How could the two students work out their relationship now that they've yelled at each other?

3. Think of some suggestions for Sally.

4. Offer Roberto some ideas for how best to deal with the situation.

5. Offer Sally suggestions for dealing with her frustration about science class.

6. Questions for discussion: What frustrates you at school? How do you work out your frustrations? Are these good ways?

LUNCH MONEY

SCENE

During free time on the playground, George, a seventh-grader who is large for his age, corners Harold, a smaller sixth-grader. George demands Harold's lunch money. Harold is clearly afraid of George but does not want to give up his lunch money.

QUESTIONS AND TASKS

1. Describe emotions you believe Harold was experiencing other than fear.

2. How would an incident like this affect your attitude toward school?

3. What is right or wrong about Harold later complaining to school officials?

4. If bystanders were present, how should they act?

Pizza Party

Scene

A group of four sixth-grade girls chat informally in their home room prior to the start of the day. Sally invites two of the girls to her birthday party to be held at the local pizza parlor. Jane, though standing with the group, is not asked to the party.

Questions and Tasks

1. What is Sally's problem?

2. What do you believe Jane was thinking and feeling during the conversation?

4. If Jane was hurt, is there anything she could do that would help?

5. Suggest some "inner" messages Jane could say to herself that might help the situation.

6. How could Sally have behaved differently?

Floor Hockey

Scene

The scene takes place in the locker room between two seventh-grade girls, Donna and Amelia. Donna played goalie both because of her lack of athletic ability and because of the fact that she does not enjoy competition. It was a close game, but Donna's team lost on a last-minute goal. Even Donna would admit that she botched what should have been an easy goal, but as is her tendency, she laughs it off. Amelia, a teammate, is infuriated and confronts her, starting the conversation with the remark that Donna is a "feeb." Donna tries to calm Amelia.

Questions and Tasks

1. Why do you think Amelia was angry?

2. What is a basic difference between the personalities of Amelia and Donna?

3. Describe how differences in the girls' personalities affected the way this scene played out.

4. Evaluate Donna's response to Amelia. Was it appropriate?

ANNOYING BOY

SCENE

As a seventh-grader, Greg has a lot going for him. He is a pleasant, easy-going person, the star of the seventh-grade football team, and finds learning very easy. John, on the other hand, is very troubled. Because of a condition that no one knows about, John has trouble controlling his behavior sometimes. Once in a while, he will make throaty noises during class. Greg has decided to talk to John about his behavior. Greg's biggest worry is that John will be hurt or that John will feel intimidated by Greg. Greg does not want John to be embarrassed or humiliated but feels it's appropriate to talk to John as one student to another. He sits down next to John at lunch and says . . .

QUESTIONS AND TASKS

1. Assuming that Greg is more popular than John, will their different social standing affect how John relates to Greg's advice?

2. Should Greg talk to John at all? Why or why not?

3. List some skills it takes to talk to someone when their behavior bothers you.

4. Did Greg display these skills?

5. Replay the scene based on the effective skills listed for #3.

HUMILIATION

SCENE

Alvin and Ray do not much care for school, except as a place to showcase how tough they are. Many of the other sixth-graders are a little frightened of them. Yesterday, Juan brought his violin to show-and-tell. This morning before school, on the playground, Alvin and Ray follow Juan around and harass him. They mock Juan by pretending to play the violin and inform him that only "fags" go in for such things. Juan knows that if he reacts too strongly, the pair will beat him up, if not now, then later. He would, however, like to defend himself. Many other students see the exchange as Juan wanders around the playground in the attempt to lose Ray and Alvin.

QUESTIONS AND TASKS

1. What do you think Juan was thinking as Alvin and Ray walked over to him?

2. Should bystanders (other students) do something? Why or why not?

3. If you think bystanders should help, what ought to be done?

4. Was Alvin's and Ray's behavior bullying?

HE GOT UP ON THE WRONG SIDE OF THE BED

SCENE

Mr. Smather is a decent math teacher, though not many students like him personally. He is a bit on the moody side and is never particularly friendly. On his good days, Mr. Smather is seen as a hard-working teacher who likes math and knows how to teach it. He is not talkative, however, and tends to be very matter-of-fact with students. On his bad days, like today, he can be a growling bear. Some of Mr. Smather's sixth-graders in the back of the room were talking while he was answering another student's question. He sincerely thought the "talkers" were Lisa and Jeffrey, so he asked them to stay after class. In the scene, Lisa denies talking out of turn and Mr. Smather "loses it." He yells at both students and accuses them of being worthless liars. Both students try to explain, but he yells over them.

QUESTIONS AND TASKS

1. Is this scene, as played, an example of bullying? Why or why not?

2. What relationship problems are faced by the students in the scene?

3. List some possible actions that Jeffrey and Lisa could take.

4. Does adult behavior in a school affect whether students bully each other? If so, how?

APPENDICES

E | ENMESHMENT CHECKLIST

ENMESHMENT CHECKLIST

1. Does the family look for satisfaction almost completely within the home?
   Yes _____   No _____

2. Does the family place a high value on words?
   Yes _____   No _____

3. Is control very important to the family?
   Yes _____   No _____

4. Does the family believe that loving means thinking and feeling exactly alike?
   Yes _____   No _____

5. Does the family believe that one person's advantage comes out of another's suffering?
   Yes _____   No _____

6. Does the family believe that selfishness is evil?
   Yes _____   No _____

7. Does the family believe that it is wrong for family members to be different and act differently?
   Yes _____   No _____

8. Does the family believe that fighting and conflict within the family is to be avoided at all costs?
   Yes _____   No _____

9. Do family members frequently speak for each other?
   Yes _____   No _____

10. Do the parents see their relationship as one of dominance and submission?
    Yes _____   No _____

APPENDICES

C

CCM CHECKLIST

COMMON CONCERN CHECKLIST (BULLY/VICTIM INTERVIEWS)
DATE _____

TASK I. PROTECTING THE VICTIM:

1. Was first-hand information obtained first and primarily from knowledgeable adults to protect the victim?   Yes ___ No ___

2. Was (were) the alleged bully(ies) interviewed first?   Yes ___ No ___

3. Was sufficient time allowed to gain information from each party involved?   Yes ___ No ___

4. Was privacy afforded to each party as needed?   Yes ___ No ___

5. Were separate interviews conducted?   Yes ___ No ___

6. Was an assessment made of the degree of safety felt by the victim and was the response adjusted accordingly?   Yes ___ No ___

7. Was the next meeting with the victim planned soon enough to best assure his or her safety?   Yes ___ No ___

8. Did the victim feel reassured and supported by the intervention? Yes ___ No ___

TASK II. FOSTERING RAPPORT AND STUDENT RELATIONSHIPS:

1. Were the room and seating arrangements conducive to talking freely and sharing openly?   Yes ___ No ___

2. In the interview(s) with the student(s), did the communication begin on equal terms?   Yes ___ No ___

3. Were the words and language used clear, understandable, and on an approximate matching level with those of the students?   Yes ___ No ___

4. Did I use posture sharing with the interviewee to further rapport development as needed?   Yes ___ No ___

5. Did I really listen fully to the student(s) and give them sufficient time to talk?   Yes ___ No ___

6. Was the message communicated successfully to the student(s) that I cared about them and the way they treat each other?   Yes ___ No ___

7. From the point of view of the student(s) involved with the intervention, do they view my actions as positive and helpful?   Yes ___ No ___

TASK III. FOSTERING EMPATHY BETWEEN BULLY(IES) AND VICTIM:

1. Did the emotional tone of the interview promote the development of empathy?   Yes ___ No ___

2. Were actions taken during the interview(s) directed at moderating the vocal tone and level of emotional reactions?   Yes ___ No ___

   a. Was the interview free of emotional outbursts and reactive emotional responses to the situation on my part?   Yes ___ No ___

   b. Was an accusatory tone avoided?   Yes ___ No ___

   c. Was a morally superior tone avoided?   Yes ___ No ___

   d. Did I resort to any put-downs in my responses to the situation?
                                                                      Yes ___ No ___

3. In conducting the interview(s), were distractions minimized as much as possible?   Yes ___ No ___

4. Was genuine concern for the victim effectively communicated to the parties involved?   Yes ___ No ___

5. Was the suspected bullying student provided an opportunity and sufficient time to reflect on the viewpoint of the victim? Yes ___ No ___

6. Was my attitude as positive as possible?   Yes ___ No ___

7. As a bridge to empathy, did I help to point out the common ground and connections that might exist between the parties?   Yes ___ No ___

8. Did I give the bullying student an opportunity to put himself or herself in the place of the victim?   Yes ___ No ___

9. Did I utilize reverse role playing strategies to foster empathy development as needed?   Yes ___ No ___

10. Was the victim informed of the bully's perspective?   Yes ___ No ___

TASK IV. SUCCESSFUL PROBLEM SOLVING:

1. Was problem solving [point #3] introduced before any empathy was expressed or implied?   Yes ___ No ___

2. Did the level of emotional intensity present during the interview impede reasoning toward a solution?   Yes ___ No ___

3. Was silence used effectively to encourage the student's problem solving, ownership of the problem, and responsibility for the outcome? Yes ___ No ___

4. Was a positive attitude on my part reflected during the interview? Yes ___ No ___

5. Did I effectively channel the emotional energy present in the interview toward constructive, problem-solving outlets? Yes ___ No ___

6. Were my positive expectations about the outcome of the interview communicated to the students? Yes ___ No ___

7. Was the plan arrived at by the students concrete and doable? Yes ___ No ___

8. Were the students informed, if appropriate, about the school's policy regarding bullying and peer harassment? Yes ___ No ___

9. Was a parent/child conference planned or considered in the problem-solving process? Yes ___ No ___

10. Was the groundwork laid for an eventual joint meeting between the bully(ies) and the victim? Yes ___ No ___

11. Was sufficient time allotted for effective problem solving by all parties involved? Yes ___ No ___

12. Were the strengths of the student(s) enlisted in the problem-solving process? Yes ___ No ___

TASK V. EVALUATING AND IMPROVING INTERVENTION EFFECTIVENESS:

1. The most effective part of the interview was:

_____
_____
_____

2. The least effective part of the interview was:

_____
_____
_____

3. To increase my effectiveness with similar situations in the future, I intend to do the following:

_____
_____
_____

CCM Checklist
(Provocative Victim Interviews)

Task I. Facilitating successful problem solving:

1. Was concern about the situation genuinely expressed and communicated by the interventionist? Yes ____ No ____

2. Was the viewpoint of the bully(ies) communicated clearly to the student? Yes ____ No ____

3. Were the strengths of the student and the positives of the situation highlighted and enlisted in the problem-solving phase of the interview? Yes ____ No ____

4. Was the interview structured to allow the victim the opportunity to gain insight into his or her role in the situation? Yes ____ No ____

5. Was the purpose of the provoking behavior assessed and identified with the help of the student? Yes ____ No ____

6. Were alternate ways of meeting this purpose or need, identified in question #5, explored with the student? Yes ____ No ____

7. Was a plan developed to better meet these needs? Yes ____ No ____

8. Was sufficient time allotted for the problem solving to be undertaken effectively? Yes ____ No ____

9. At the conclusion of the interview, was the provoking behavior clearly identified and explained in an understandable way to the student? Yes ____ No ____

10. If the Suggestive Command Method (SCM) was used, was there a sound reason for preempting the student? Yes ____ No ____

Task II. Improving intervention outcomes:

1. The most effective words/actions I used during the interview were:

_____

_____

_____

2. The least effective words/actions I used during the interview were:

_____

_____

_____

3. To be more effective in the future, I need to:

_____

_____

_____

EARLY INTERVENTION REMINDER CHECKLIST (GROUP FOLLOW-UP WORK)

TASK I. FACILITATING SUCCESSFUL GROUP PROBLEM SOLVING:

1. Was the victim appropriately excluded from the first meeting with the bullies? Yes ___ No ___

2. Was responsibility for the session's outcome placed directly in the hands of the students? Yes ___ No ___

3. Did I avoid rescuing actions? Yes ___ No ___

4. If yes on question #3, was it used effectively? Yes ___ No ___

5. Were the positives of the situation and the strengths of the students highlighted and enlisted? Yes ___ No ___

6. Was silence used effectively to encourage empathy with the victim and effective problem solving? Yes ___ No ___

7. Was the broken-record method used appropriately to encourage problem solving? Yes ___ No ___

8. Did I avoid being drawn into the role of a prosecutor or judge during the session? Yes ___ No ___

9. Was the importance of mutual tolerance and peaceful coexistence communicated to the students? Yes ___ No ___

10. Were any disputes between the participants successfully mediated by the interventionist? Yes ___ No ___

11. Was the group prepared and the groundwork laid for future joint problem-solving work with the victims? Yes ___ No ___

12. Were all the participants given time and opportunity for problem solving? Yes ___ No ___

TASK II. IMPROVING GROUP OUTCOMES:

1. The most effective words/actions I used during the interview were:

_____

_____

_____

2. The least effective words/actions I used during the interview were:

_____

_____

_____

3. To be more effective in the future, I need to:

_____

_____

_____

APPENDICES

LIST OF RESOURCES RELATED TO BULLYING

LIST OF RESOURCES RELATED TO BULLYING

Albert, D.H. (1985). *People Power: Applying Nonviolence Theory*. Philadelphia: New Society Publishers.

American Association of University Women (with Lewis Harris and Associates). (1993). Hostile Hallways: The AAUW Survey on Sexual Harassment in America's Schools. Write to: AAUW Sales Office, P.O. Box 251, Annapolis Jct., MD 20701-0251.

Bellanca, J. (1991). *Blueprints for Thinking in the Cooperative Classroom*. Palatine, IL: Skylight Publishers.

Besay, V. (Undated). *Bullies and Victims in Schools: A Guide to Understanding and Management*. Philadelphia: Taylor and Francis.

Brody, E. (Ed.) (1992). *Spinning Tales, Weaving Hope: Stories of Peace, Justice & the Environment*. Philadelphia: New Society Publishers.
This is a collection of twenty-nine stories and includes suggested follow-up activities and ways of improving one's story-telling ability.

Brown, T. (Undated). *The Broken Toy* [videotape]. Zanesville, OH: Summerhill Productions. "Toy" is a deeply moving story that deals with the life-threatening consequences of a bullying episode. Despite rather poor production values, we find this to be a powerful story, well told. We recommend that it be used with students over third grade and that young people seeing the tape have a chance to deal with emotional issues it raises with responsible adults. Highly recommended.

Carlsson-Page, N., & Levin, D. (1990). *Who's Calling the Shots? How to Respond Effectively to Children's Fascination with War Play and War Toys*. Philadelphia: New Society Publishers.
The role of aggressive play is examined in children, and alternatives to war toys are suggested.

Clark, A.J., & Seals, J.M. (1984). Group Counseling for Ridiculed Children. *Journal of Specialists in Group Work, 9*(3), 157–160.

Crago, H. (1986). The Place of Story in Affective Development: Implications for Educators and Clinicians. *Journal of Children in Contemporary Society, 17*(4), 129-142.

Crum, T.F (1987). *Magic of Conflict*. New York: Simon & Schuster.
Crum explores the philosophy of Aikido for presenting conflict as an opportunity for choice and change.

Derman-Sparks, L. (1989). *Anti-bias Curriculum: Tools for Empowering Young Children*. Washington, DC: National Association for the Education of Young Children.
For those who work with children two years and older, this book provides a valuable guide with resource material.

Foster, E. (1989). *Energizers and Icebreakers.* Minneapolis: Educational Media Corporation.
A variety of activities are described to promote a friendly, cooperative group atmosphere.

Fry-Miller, K., & Myers-Walls, J. (1988). *Young Peacemakers Project Book.* Ashland, OR: Brethren Press.
This book and its sequel, *Peace Works,* offer hours of fun and constructive activities for young children.

Gabelko, N. (1981). *Reducing Adolescent Prejudice: A Handbook of the Anti-Defamation League of B'nai B'rith.* New York: Teacher's College Press.
This handbook presents learning activities intended to increase critical thinking ability and moral reasoning for secondary students.

Garrity, C., Jens, K., Porter, W., Sager, N., & Short-Camilli, C. (1995). *Bully Proofing Your School: A Comprehensive Approach for Elementary Schools.* Longmont, CO: Sopris West.
"Bully proofing" is a comprehensive anti-bullying program designed for use in elementary schools and is somewhat based on Olweus's work in Norway. It is an excellent program, complete with discussion notes, overhead transparency masters, and ideas for buttons and posters.

Gibbs, J. (1987). *Tribes: A Process for Social Development & Cooperative Learning.* Santa Rosa, CA: Center-Source Publications.
This book will help teach interaction skills, responsible behavior, mutual rewarding measures, and genuine regard for self and others.

Gifaldi, D. (1986). *One Thing for Sure.* New York: Clarion Books.

Gittler, J. (Ed.) (1989). *Annual Review of Conflict Knowledge & Conflict Resolution.* New York: Garland Publishing.
This books reviews the field of interpersonal, ethnic, and other forms of conflict in a systematic and comprehensive manner.

Hoover, J.H. (in press). *Schoolyard Bullying.* York, PA: The William Gladden Foundation.
This is a small pamphlet that contains much of the information from chapters 1 and 2 of this book in a question-and-answer format.

Jampolsky, G. (Ed.) (1982). *Children as Teachers of Peace.* Berkeley, CA: Celestial Arts.
This book provides drawings, essays, and letters by children. It contains a wealth of ideas for activities.

Keen, S. (1991). *Faces of the Enemy: Reflections of the Hostile Imagination.* New York: Harper.
Keen looks at the forces that legitimize violence against whatever group is now considered the enemy through verbal bullying (i.e., propaganda).

Kreidler, W.J. (1984). *Creative Conflict Resolution: More Than 200 Activities for Keeping Peace in the Classroom, K-6.* New York: Scott, Foresman & Company.

McCollough, C. (1991). *Resolving Conflict with Justice and Peace.* Pilgrim Press.
Written by a United Church of Christ minister, this book combines theoretical and philosophical factors with applied examples.

Miedzian, M. (1991). *Boys Will Be Boys: Breaking the Link Between Masculinity and Violence.* New York: Doubleday.
This social scientist explores the implications of equating masculinity and violence and suggests alternative measures and fresh thinking.

Miller, M. (1992). *Coping with a Bigoted Parent.* New York: Rosen Publishing Group.
This book is part of the "Coping with" series designed to provide young adults with guidance in dealing with difficult problems.

Montuori, A., & Conti, I. (1993). *From Power to Partnership.* New York: Harper.
The principles of social theorist Riane Eisler, author of *The Chalice and the Blade*, are spelled out in constructing an alternative model to explain today's complex choices.

National School Safety Center (Undated). *Set Straight on Bullies* [videotape]. Westlake Village, CA: National School Safety Center.
We find this film to be an excellent conversation starter. It can be used with parents, teachers, and older students. It tells the story of how a bullying incident led to a plan to improve the climate in a middle school. It can be ordered from The National School Safety Center, 4165 Thousand Oaks Blvd., Suite 290, Westlake Village, CA 91362.

Oliver, R.L., Young, T.A., & LaSalle, S.M. (1994). Bullying and Victimization: The Help and Hindrance of Children's Literature. *The School Counselor, 42,* 137–146.

Olweus, D. (1991). Bullying at School: What We Know and What We Can Do. Department of Psychosocial Science, University of Bergen, Oysteinsgate 3, N 5007, Bergen, Norway. Phone: 475 212327.

Rochman, H. (1993). *Against Borders: Promoting Books for a Multicultural World.* Chicago: American Library Association.

Teaching Tolerance. Southern Poverty Law Center Periodical.
Articles, resource lists, and letters in this practical magazine are helpful material for teachers.

Wade, R. (1991). *Joining Hands: From Personal to Planetary Friendship in the Primary Classroom.* Tucson, AZ: Zephyr Press.

Webster-Doyle, T. (1991). *Why Is Everybody Always Picking on Me? A Guide to Understanding Bullies.* Middlebury, CT: Atrium Society.
A host of nonviolent solutions are given, activities offered, and insight into the bully and victim dynamic afforded. The author notes the cultural push to passively conform while pulled to aggressively succeed and comes to view bullying as a reflection of a self-centered, violent lifestyle choice.

Weinstein, M. (1990). *Playfair: Everybody's Guide to Noncompetitive Play.* San Luis Obispo, CA: Impact Publishers.
Activities and games for all ages, designed to encourage cooperation.

Wichert, S. (1989). *Keeping the Peace: Practicing Cooperation and Conflict Resolution with Preschoolers.* Philadelphia: New Society Publishers.

(Note: Our thanks to Ruth Weins and the Readers' Services Department of the Tulsa Central Library for help with this search.)

APPENDICES

T

TEASING DISCUSSION QUESTIONS

TEASING: QUESTIONS FOR DISCUSSION

1. What is teasing?

2. What is bullying?

3. Does teasing fit your definition of bullying?

4. When (if ever) is teasing not bullying?

5. How can you tell if a person likes it when you tease them?

6. How can you tell when a person being teased is bothered?

7. Are there "signals" that a teasing statement is meant playfully and not to hurt?

8. A person makes it clear that teasing on a certain subject (like being overweight) hurts their feelings. Should you stop? Why or why not?

9. Are there reasons to continue teasing someone even if they don't like it?

10. Why do some kids tease even when others don't like it?

11. List some ways you could get others to quit teasing you.

12. Bob is teasing Bill, and Bill is bothered.

    a. Should bystanders (other kids watching) do anything? Why or why not?

    b. What, if anything, could bystanders do to help the situation?

13. What is harassment?

14. Is harassment different from teasing?

15. Would you like to know more about teasing?

APPENDICES

T

TEASING DOs AND DON'Ts

Teasing DOs and DON'Ts

DO:

1. Be careful of others' feelings.

2. Use humor gently and carefully.

3. Ask whether teasing about a certain topic hurts someone's feelings.

4. Accept teasing from others if you tease.

5. Tell others if teasing about a certain topic hurts your feelings.

6. Know the difference between friendly gentle teasing and hurtful ridicule or harassment.

7. Try to read others' "body language" to see if their feelings are hurt—even when they don't tell you.

8. Help a weaker student when he or she is being ridiculed.

DON'T:

1. Tease someone you don't know well.

2. [If you are a boy] tease girls about sex.

3. Tease about a person's body.

4. Tease about a person's family members.

5. Tease about a topic when a student has asked you not to.

6. Tease someone who seems agitated or who you know is having a bad day.

7. Be thin-skinned about teasing that is meant in a friendly way.

8. Swallow your feelings about teasing—tell someone in a direct and clear way what is bothering you.

APPENDICES

C

A BRIEF SCREENING CHECKLIST FOR FAMILIES OF BULLIES

A BRIEF SCREENING CHECKLIST FOR FAMILIES OF BULLIES*

Instructions. For each item below, check the most accurate response.

1. Does the parent, or parents, clearly hold executive decision-making authority in the family?

   Yes _____   No _____

2. Are the rules of the household known by the family members, and do the rules reflect humane and developmentally appropriate expectations?

   Yes _____   No _____

3. Is the communication between family members direct, clear, free, and relatively spontaneous?

   Yes _____   No _____

4. Is the family able to come to some agreement on defining the problem behavior that needs to change and suggest possible solutions?

   Yes _____   No _____

5. Has the family dealt successfully in the past with any related problems or issues?

   Yes _____   No _____

6. Is the family able to follow through and complete an agreed-upon family task?

   Yes _____   No _____

7. Does the family expect a positive outcome to the present problem?

   Yes _____   No _____

8. Is there reason to suspect that the child is a victim of parental child abuse or neglect?

   Yes _____   No _____

DECISION TREE:

Are there two or more "No" answers above?
If so, then referral is indicated.

Is the answer to question 8 "Yes?"
If so, then referral is indicated.

*This checklist was adapted from earlier work by Golden, L.B. (1988).

About *The Bullying Prevention Handbook* and the National Educational Service

The mission of the National Educational Service is to provide tested and proven resources that help those who work with youth create safe and caring schools, agencies, and communities where all children succeed. *The Bullying Prevention Handbook* is just one of many resources and staff development opportunities NES provides that focus on building a community circle of caring. If you have any questions, comments, articles, manuscripts, or youth art you would like us to consider for publication, please contact us at the address below.

Staff Development Opportunities Include:

Integrating Technology Effectively
Improving Schools through Quality Leadership
Creating Professional Learning Communities
Building Cultural Bridges
Discipline with Dignity
Ensuring Safe Schools
Managing Disruptive Behavior
Reclaiming Youth At Risk
Working with Today's Families

National Educational Service
1252 Loesch Road
Bloomington, IN 47404
(812) 336-7700
(800) 733-6786 (toll free number)
FAX (812) 336-7790
e-mail: nes@nesonline.com
www.nesonline.com

NEED MORE COPIES OR ADDITIONAL RESOURCES ON THIS TOPIC?

Need more copies of this book? Want your own copy? Need additional resources on this topic? If so, you can order additional materials by using this form or by calling us toll free at (800) 733-6786 or (812) 336-7700. Or you can order by FAX at (812) 336-7790, or visit our website: www.nesonline.com.

Title	Price*	Quantity	Total
The Bullying Prevention Handbook	$ 23.95		
Set Straight on Bullies (video and Facilitator's Guide)	139.00		
Reconnecting Youth: A Peer Group Approach to Building Life Skills	179.00		
Anger Management for Youth: Stemming Aggression and Violence	24.95		
Containing Crisis: A Guide for Managing School Emergencies	19.95		
Youth Suicide: A Comprehensive Manual for Prevention and Intervention	19.95		
Achievement for African-American Students: Strategies for the Diverse Classroom	21.95		
From Rage to Hope: Strategies for Reclaiming Black and Hispanic Students	21.95		
Safe Schools: A Handbook for Violence Prevention	29.95		
Dealing with Youth Violence: What Schools and Communities Need to Know	18.95		
Breaking the Cycle of Violence (two-video set and Leader's Guide)	239.00		
What Do I Do When...? How to Achieve Discipline with Dignity in the Classroom	21.95		
Discipline with Dignity (three-video set and Comprehensive Guide)	356.00		
SUBTOTAL			
Shipping: Add 5% of order total. For orders outside the continental U.S., add 7% of order total.			
Handling: Add $3.00. For orders outside the continental U.S., add $5.00.			
TOTAL			

*Prices subject to change without notice.

❏ Check enclosed   ❏ Purchase order enclosed

❏ Money order   ❏ VISA, MasterCard, Discover, or American Express

Credit Card No._____ Exp. Date _____

Cardholder Signature _____

SHIP TO:

Name_____ Position_____

Institution _____

Address _____

City_____ State_____ ZIP _____

Phone_____ FAX _____

E-mail _____

National Educational Service
1252 Loesch Road
Bloomington, IN 47404
(812) 336-7700 • (800) 733-6786 (toll free number)
FAX (812) 336-7790
e-mail: nes@nesonline.com • www.nesonline.com